# Preaching
# Through the Bible

## Genesis 12–23

### Michael Eaton

**Sovereign World**

Sovereign World
PO Box 777
Tonbridge
Kent, TN11 0ZS
England

*By the same author:*
*Ecclesiastes* (Tyndale Commentary) – IVP
*Living A Godly Life* – Paternoster
*Living Under Grace* (Romans 6–7) – Paternoster
*Predestination and Israel* (Romans 9–11) – Paternoster
*Enjoying God's Worldwide Church* – Paternoster
*A Theology of Encouragement* – Paternoster
*Applying God's Law* – Paternoster
*1 Samuel* (Preaching Through the Bible) – Sovereign World
*2 Samuel* (Preaching Through the Bible) – Sovereign World
*1, 2 Thessalonians* (Preaching Through the Bible) – Sovereign World
*Mark* (Preaching Through the Bible) – Sovereign World
*Genesis 1–11* (Preaching Through the Bible) – Sovereign World
*1, 2, 3 John* (Focus on the Bible) – Christian Focus
*Hosea* (Focus on the Bible) – Christian Focus
*Experiencing God* – Paternoster
*Joel and Amos* (Preaching Through the Bible) – Sovereign World

ISBN: 1-85240-244-X

Typeset by CRB Associates, Reepham, Norfolk
Printed in Great Britain by Cox & Wyman Ltd, Reading, Berkshire

# Preface

There is need of a series of biblical expositions which are especially appropriate for English-speaking people throughout the world. Such expositions need to be laid out in such a way that they will be useful to those who like to have their material or (if they are preachers) to put across their material in clear points. They need to avoid difficult vocabulary and advanced grammatical structures. They need to avoid European or North American illustrations. *Preaching Through the Bible* seeks to meet such a need. Although intended for an international audience I have no doubt that their simplicity will be of interest to many first-language speakers of English as well. These expositions are based upon the Hebrew and Greek texts. The New American Standard Version and the New International Version of the Bible are recommended for the reader but at times the expositor will simply translate the Hebrew or Greek himself.

The origin of each of these volumes is to be found in the preaching of God's Word. It is not our purpose to deal with minute exegetical detail, although the commentator has to do work of this nature as part of his preliminary preparation. But just as a housewife likes to serve a good meal rather than display her pots and pans, so we are concerned with the 'good meal' of Scripture, rather than the 'pots and pans' of dictionaries, disputed interpretations and the like. Only occasionally will such matters have to be discussed. Similarly matters of 'Introduction' receive only as much attention as is necessary for the exposition to be clear. Although on the surface written simply these expositions aim at a high level of scholarship, and attempt to put the theological and practical message of each book of the Bible in a clear and practical manner. A simple outline of some 'introductory' matters is to be found in the first chapter of this second book, but then we get straight into the message of the story of Abraham.

*Michael A. Eaton*

# Contents

## Contents

**Maps**

# Author's Preface

This second little book on Genesis, like the previous one, has arisen from my experience of preaching through this part of the Bible. I first preached through the story of Abraham in Rouxville Baptist Church, Johannesburg, some years ago. Later I gave expositions of the whole of Genesis on Trans-World Radio. Then in 1996 I preached again through the story of Abraham in various fellowships in Nairobi. These chapters constitute notes on my preaching at that time.

I am grateful, as always, to family and friends who encourage my preaching. Thanks to Chris Mungeam for his enthusiasm and zeal for God's work, to my family, Jenny, Tina Gysling, my daughter, who works through my material, Calvin who, when computers gnash their teeth, rescues my soul from their destructions, and whose comments on my expositions often get added to these pages.

*Michael A. Eaton*

# Chapter 1

## Introducing Abram
### (Genesis 11:27–12:1)

The first five books of the Bible are a united set of writings. They are really one set of books in three sections. Genesis tells the story of creation, sin, and salvation by faith. The three middle books (Exodus–Numbers) tell the main story of Israel's redemption by the blood of a lamb. Deuteronomy is a record of Moses' preaching just before Israel went into the land of Canaan. It presses home some lessons that arise from the central story in Exodus to Numbers.

It will help us if we get an overview. The first five books of the Bible unfold like this:

**Part 1. The Prehistory of Israel's Redemption (Genesis)**
 The Creation of Everything (1:1–2:3)
 The Offspring of Heaven and Earth (2:4–4:26)
 The 'Book' of the Offspring of Adam (5:1–6:8)
 The Offspring of Noah (6:9–9:29)
 The Offspring of the Sons of Noah (10:1–11:9)
 The Offspring of Shem (11:10–26)
 The Succession of Terah (11:27–25:11)
 The Offspring of Ishmael (25:12–18)
 The Offspring of Isaac (25:19–35:29)
 The Offspring of Edom (36:1–43)
 The Offspring of Jacob (37:1–50:26)

**Part 2. The Redemption of Israel (Exodus–Numbers)**
 Redemption By the Blood of a Lamb
  (Exodus 1:1–15:21)
 Establishment of Israel as the People of God
  (Exodus 15:22–40:38)
 Law and Ordinances of the Sinai-Covenant (Leviticus)
 Journeying From Sinai to Moab (Numbers)

**Part 3. Moses' Reminders and Exhortations (Deuteronomy)**
Preamble (1:1–5)
Historical Prologue (1:6–4:49)
Stipulations: Covenant Life (5:1–26:19)
Sanctions and Covenant Ratification (27:1–30:20)
Arrangements for the Future (31:1–34:20)

Everything in Genesis 1:1–11:26 goes back to the days before Abraham. The stories of Genesis 1–11 may have been family tradition brought by Abraham from Mesopotamia where the family originally lived. Genesis 11:27–50:26 are the family traditions of Abraham, Isaac, Jacob and Joseph. Some time later Moses did a lot of writing. He wrote accounts of the doom of Amalek (Exodus 17:14) and the documents of the covenant at Sinai. Much or all of the legislation of Leviticus comes from this period. Records of the journeys of the Israelites were kept. So at about the time of the entry of Israel into the land of Canaan, most of what we call the first five books of the Bible was already in existence. They became known as 'the books of Moses'.

This does not mean that Moses produced it in the precise form that we have it. There is evidence that the first five books of the Bible, Genesis–Deuteronomy, were edited and compiled somewhere between the days of Moses and the days of the kings of Israel. It was certainly put together after Moses' death. And Genesis 36:11 clearly was written after kings reigned in Israel, that is, after the days of Saul and David. Solomon's times were days of literary work and it is likely that during these days Genesis reached its present form. It seems then that our Genesis was drafted around 1300 BC from earlier materials but came to its final form, as we have it in Hebrew, about 950 BC. We notice that Genesis has ten 'markers' or internal headings (2:4; 5:1; 6:9; 10:1; 11:10, 27; 25:12, 19; 36:1; 37:1). These headings are quite deliberate and were placed there by the editor of this material, to divide the book into sections in the way analysed above.

The first eleven chapters dealt with creation, the fall into sin and the calamity that came upon the human race. God brought into being a new world out of the waters of the flood and re-started the world under different conditions. Sin and death were still present but God spread the nations throughout the ancient world and got ready to introduce Abraham.

The remainder of Genesis shows us how faith works by exhibiting the life of faith in the stories of Abraham (11:27–25:11), Ishmael, Isaac, Jacob and Esau (25:12–36:43), and then in the story of Joseph which is given special attention (37:2–50:20). Joseph's story shows us how the life of faith works out in one more of Abraham's descendants, but at the same time explains how Israel came to be in Egypt and so in need of salvation by the blood of a lamb.

We are ready, then, for the story of Abraham. The main point is this: **Abraham was a model of faith**.

He is the model of saving faith. We are 'justified', that is declared righteous before God, in the same way that Abraham was justified. Abraham was the model of justification for the apostle Paul.

Abraham is the model of diligent faith. It is by persisting in faith that we inherit God's promises. Initial faith brings us into being right with God. Persistent faith inherits God's promises.

Abraham is the model of freedom from the law. He lived before the Mosaic law existed. He did everything that he did without the use of the Mosaic law.

Abraham is the model of hearing God's voice. Abraham did not have the law and he did not even have the Bible! Yet he heard from God. He had a personal experience of God and knew that God was speaking to him. Abraham is the model of justification by works. Decades after he was justified he reached a high level of obedience and became pleasing to God. After his obedience was severely tested God said to him 'I know that you are righteous'. James calls this 'justification by works'. It has nothing to do with our first salvation. It has nothing to do with Paul's phrase 'justification by faith'. It refers to the highest level of pleasing God. Once again, Abraham is the model.

Abraham is the model of living on a high-priest. In a time of great conflict, when he was supremely weary, he found blessing from a great high priest, Melchizedek. He represents

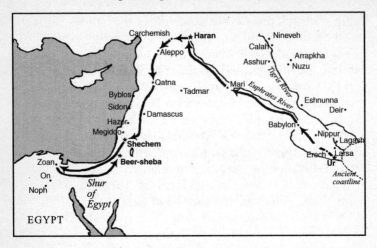

***Map 1*** *Abram's journey to Canaan.*

to us our living on a great High Priest after the order of Melchizedek.

Abraham is the model of what it means to experience God's oath. 'I swear that I will bless you', said God to Abraham. It all began when Abraham heard God's call and started believing God.

# Chapter 2

## Believing God

(Genesis 11:27–12:1)

Abraham is the greatest figure in the Bible, after Jesus. The biblical story in Genesis 1–11 swiftly leads to him. God created the world in perfection (1:1–2:3). Man and woman were the climax of creation (2:4–25). Soon, however, inspired by 'the snake' they tried to be like gods (3:1–7) and the result was shame, guilt, loss of innocence and exclusion from paradise (3:8–24).

One might think that human beings would never sin again, but the fall of the human race was more serious than that, and sin had become part of their nature. Having sinned in the garden of Eden, man sinned outside the garden of Eden as well. Soon demonic powers of some kind were entering into intimate relationship with the human race (6:1–8). The result was awful depravity and God decided to destroy humankind from 'the world' and begin again with Noah. Even the flood did not restrain human sin for very long. Soon men were trying again to climb into heaven by their own devices (11:1–9). Innocence had failed (Genesis 1–3). Exclusion from paradise brought no worldwide repentance (Genesis 4–6). The exterminating flood led to no new humanity in any deep sense (Genesis 6–11). Depravity was on the increase. It was the right time for God to introduce His major initiative in fulfilling the promise of Genesis 3:15 that He would crush 'the snake' and everything that he had done. He had promised worldwide blessing through someone in the line of Shem (Genesis 9:27).

God chose Abraham – or Abram as he was called at this point. He was an idolater from the moon-worshipping cities

15

of Ur and Haran. But just as Noah had 'found grace', Abram too had 'found grace' and had been chosen by God to be the initiator of God's programme of salvation. God stepped into his life. There was no special preparation in the life of Abram. The story is abrupt and startling; the initiative was entirely on God's side. The voice of God came to a pagan man living in Ur, a city in which the 'Chaldean' tribe lived. (Later, the 'Chaldeans' inhabited Babylon and the word 'Chaldean' meant 'Babylonian', as in the Hebrew of Habakkuk 1:6.)

This is typical of the Bible's teaching about grace. God chose Abram, setting His love on him and determining that he should be summoned to salvation and used by God. *'Those whom God foreknew He also predestined'* (see Romans 8:29). Abram was chosen before the foundation of the world (see Ephesians 1:4–5), predestined to an inheritance (see Ephesians 1:11). Before he was born God had set His heart on him (like Jeremiah and Paul; see Jeremiah 1:5; Galatians 1:15).

Terah, Abram's father, had at least two wives (Genesis 20:12). Haran and Nahor were apparently, Abram's elder brothers. At some time before Abram was 75 years old, Terah left Ur. The son Haran married in Ur and had two daughters, but then died at a time when the family were still living in Ur. Nahor married one of his nieces. Abram married his half-sister, Sarai.

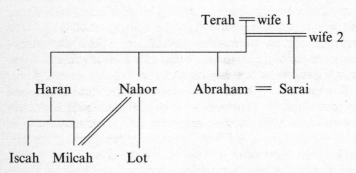

At some time before Abram's seventy-fifth year the family moved to Haran. Then Terah died; Abram was about 75 years old (Acts 7:4). Long before he been called to leave Ur (see

Acts 7:4; Genesis 15:6), but it was only after Terah's death that there was opportunity for him to follow God's summons. Abram was called to keep travelling. He took with him Sarai and Lot.

He was called to a life of **faith**. God had come to him in Ur. *'Now Yahweh said to Abram ...'*. Genesis 15:7 makes it clear that it happened in Ur. *'I am Yahweh who brought you from Ur ...'*. This is why some translations have 'The LORD **had** said ...'. On God's side Abram's story began with God's predestination. On Abram's side, all of Abram's blessings came to him by faith, when God spoke to him.

1. **Faith is based on a revelation of God's will**. *'Now Yahweh said ...'*. It is not possible to have faith unless there is some kind of revelation. Faith is faith in something that God has said. It is not a 'natural' ability that all people have that can be 'switched on'. Faith is always faith in some kind of word or revelation from God.

Abram is the model man of faith (Romans 4:16) and all believers are 'children of Abram'. But Abram's faith was faith **in what God had spoken**. *'Against hope but in hope Abraham believed in order that he would become a father of many nations, according to what had been spoken, "So shall your seed be"'* (Romans 4:18). This is a very important matter. Many strange 'faith-teachings' go astray because they do not see that **faith always relates to what God has said**. Faith is believing God, taking God at His word. If God has not given a word about any particular matter it is not possible to exercise faith. The essence of faith is to be able to say: 'I believe God, that it shall be just as it has been spoken to me' (Acts 27:25). If it has not been spoken it cannot be believed.

It is true that faith sometimes can take the form of spiritual instinct (I think 1 Samuel 14:6–14 is an example); and faith sometimes is trusting more generally in the character of God (Matthew 8:5–10 and 15:27–28 are examples), but ordinarily faith has to have some kind of 'word' from God.

If we try to 'claim' something when we have no word from God, we shall be in trouble. By faith Joshua destroyed Jericho. He did it because he was **told** to march round it for seven days blowing trumpets. If we were to march around a city for seven days blowing trumpets nothing would happen! We probably have not been given that precise word from God. By faith Enoch skipped his funeral (Hebrews 11:5), but if you were to try to go to heaven without dying you might find out you cannot take what God is not giving! We need a word from God. Then we can believe that word and 'inherit' it.

# Chapter 3

## The Promises of God
### (Genesis 12:2–3)

2. Next, we see that **faith is intensely personal**. 'Get yourself away from your country' (the Hebrew emphasizes Abram's personal responsibility). Abram must think for himself and act for himself.

> '"Go forth from your country,
> and from your relatives
> and from your father's house..."'     (12:1)

The word 'you' is a singular word; it refers to Abram only.

> '"...Go forth...
> to the land which I will show you;
> and I will make you a great nation,
> and I will bless you,
> and I will make your name great;
> and so you shall be a blessing;
> and I will bless those who bless you,
> and the one who curses you I will curse.
> And in you all the families of the earth
> shall be blessed."'     (12:1–3)

Actually hundreds of people went with Abram. He had flocks of sheep and employed herdsman (13:7). He could raise a private army (14:14). Abram's people were like a small tribe. He had a wife, who travelled with him; and Lot went also (13:1). Yet God spoke to Abram very personally. Each person has to believe for himself. Each person has to hear God's voice for himself. It is true that faith leads us into fellowship with others who also take God at His word. But there is a personal and individual side to the matter as well. Each person has to be 'convinced in his own mind' (Romans 14:5).

19

3. **Faith focuses especially on the promises of God**. When God spoke to Abram there were many promises which were given to him. There are eight phrases which have promises in them. We have reference to (i) *'... the land which I will show you...'*. God says (ii) *'...I will make you a ... nation'* (iii) *'...I will bless you'* (iv) *'...I will make your name great'* (v) *'... you shall be a blessing'* (vi) *'...I will bless those who bless you'* (vii) *'... the one who curses you I will curse'* (viii) *'... in you all the families ... shall be blessed'*.

God's Word has testimonies, precepts and promises. God testifies to the truth. He tells things the way they really are. His Word has 'testimonies'.

God gives commands. He gives orders and lays upon us what is good and right for us. His Word has 'precepts'.

God gives declarations about what God will do, He tells us what it is He wishes to do for us. His Word has 'promises'.

Testimony to facts, words requiring obedience, promises concerning God's will for the future – all of these are to be found in God's word to us. But faith especially focuses on God's promises. There are *'very great and precious promises'* (2 Peter 1:4).

4. **Faith requires patience**. All of these promises of God to Abram will require patience. The future tenses, 'I will ... I will...', do not refer to the immediate future. They do not mean 'I will instantly...'; they mean 'I will eventually...'. It is by faith and patience that Abram will inherit the promises.

5. This means too that **faith and hope are closely linked**. 'Hope' – in the way the Bible uses the word – is faith looking forward. *'Faith is being sure of what we hope for'* (Hebrews 11:1). Abram from this point onwards was expecting certain things to happen. God has spoken; Abram has believed Him.

6. **Faith may have to surmount great obstacles**. God has told Abram that he will have a land and that he will have descendants. Yet we have already been told *'Sarah was barren'* (Genesis 11:30); and *'The Canaanites were in the land'* (12:6). The land is occupied by wicked people.

Let us turn aside for a while and take a closer look at these promises which were given to Abram. In one way or another all of them can be taken to heart by the Christian. All

Christians are *'Abraham's seed, heirs according to promise'*. What is promised to Abraham is promised to his seed. What he inherits, we shall inherit.

The promises to Abram really amount to seven: (i) land, (ii) multiplication into nationhood, (iii) personal blessing, (iv) a name, (v) usefulness to God, (vi) significance, (vii) international impact. All of them depend on faith. *'Go forth . . . '*, says God, *'and I will . . . '* do this and that. If Abram does not 'Go forth', there will be no inheriting the promises.

The New Testament says that the Christian, when he comes to salvation, receives 'the promise of Abraham'. Supremely, the 'promise of Abraham' is the gift of the Holy Spirit, as Galatians 3:14 goes on to say. Yet, actually, all of the promises of Genesis 12:2–3 apply to the modern Christian in one way or another.

Think of the various ingredients in the promise that was given to Abram. One of them concerned **land**. *'Go forth . . . to the land which I will show you'*. Abram was being offered physical territory; 'the land' would later be called the land of 'Israel'. Yet the promise is a full and rich one. Actually Abram never did get much territory during his lifetime. A burial ground for his wife was all he ever got!

Abram got the enjoyment of the land. He spent the rest of his life (apart from one disastrous trip to Egypt) in Canaan. He may not have owned it but he lived as if he did!

He got a spiritual work to do for God while he was in the land of Israel. He pioneered a nation for God even before his family owned any land. There was a 'territory' for him to conquer, a realm which he had to occupy for God. The literal possession of land would come later, but the task, the area of work into which he was called, was there from the beginning.

Abram received a heavenly kingdom. Hebrews 11:16 says he was looking for a heavenly country.

One day Abram will inherit the earth. Romans 4:11 is right to say that Abraham had a promise that he would 'inherit the world'. Actually words like this are not explicit in Genesis, but Paul is drawing out the full implications of what the promise of 'land' involved.

All of these things apply to the Christian also. The

Christian in a sense 'gets land' even in this world. Although he may not own any physical territory, God sees to it that as we live by faith we enjoy God's world. *'Blessed are the meek'*, said Jesus, *'for they shall inherit the earth'*. It starts even in this life.

The Christian also has what we can call a spiritual 'territory', a realm which we have to occupy for God, a calling.

The Christian inherits a spiritual kingdom. As he moves around this world he has the presence of God with him. The Spirit is at work in his life. He inherits joy and peace, liberty and boldness. There is a spiritual kingdom at work within him as he serves God in this world. He is 'inheriting the earth'.

One day the Christian will inherit the earth, quite literally. There will quite literally be a new heavens and a new earth in which righteousness dwells. The ultimate inheritance is that every Christian will enjoy a resurrected glorified body, and will walk around in God's glorified world. In that day 'the land that I will show you' will truly have arrived and we shall have arrived in it.

# Chapter 4

## A Great Name

(Genesis 12:2–3)

The promises to Abraham are very rich and full. It will take the whole of world-history for them to be worked out and fulfilled. Abram was promised **multiplication into nationhood**. All believers are a 'great' nation; great in their worldwide extent, great in their spiritual character, great in their agreed way of godly living.

The promise was fulfilled in more than one way. A number of nations traced their descent to Abram. The Israelites, the twelve Ishmaelite tribes (see 17:20; 18:18; 21:18; 25:13–16) and the Edomites could all trace their ancestry to Abram. But Israel supremely is regarded in the Old Testament as the nation descending from Abram. God multiplied Abram until his people became a nation.

But the promise is true at another level. A spiritual nation came into being also, consisting of all those who like Abram had put their trust in the seed of Abram, Jesus. Paul argues in Romans 4 that Abraham is the father of believing Gentiles as well as of Jews.

Multiplication is part of the promise to Christians who persist in faith. It is a mistake to think that 'numbers do not matter'. Numbers do matter. On the day of Pentecost when thousands were being saved, someone was counting (Acts 2:41)! It was being added to each day (Acts 2:47), and soon *'the number of the men were about five thousand'* (Acts 4:4). The numerical growth was a vital concern. Where there is diligent faith, where there is a true walking in the Spirit, we can expect to see the people of Abraham, true believers, being multiplied. This promise, like other parts of the promise to

Abraham, also relates to the Christian. The Christian is intended to influence others. The follower of Jesus is a 'fisher of people'. He will attract others to be like him, and thus he will multiply himself. An ever-increasing spiritual nation is coming into being under the kingship of Jesus. God is still giving Abraham spiritual children.

Abram was also promised **personal blessing**. *'And I will bless you'*, said God. There would be a spiritual and a material side to the blessing. On the one side, it would include for Abram such things as long life, wealth, peace, good harvests, plenty of children. For Abram, these tangible blessings would be the indication that God was giving him favour and was with him. Spiritually it involved a place in God's plan for the world, a ministry to God's people, access into the mind of God, spiritual understanding, and the peace and joy that flows from being in the will of God.

The material side of God's 'blessing' was emphasized before Pentecost, for God's people were an earthly, political, nation. Even at that time however, the promise of material blessing always was a rough generalisation. The book of Job made the point that there could be exceptions to the rule. Under the New Covenant the emphasis changes and 'blessing' is not so much earthly wealth as *'all spiritual blessings'* (Ephesians 1:3). The phrase *'all spiritual blessings'* in Ephesians 1:3 is expounded in Ephesians 1:4–14, and the emphasis is not purely material or financial. ('Prosperity' teachers have to use the Old Testament and the Mosaic law to get across their teaching. Apart from a few favourite verses there is not much in the epistles that they can use.) 'Blessing' still includes the provision of all needs (see Philippians 4:19 which has been talking about money, Philippians 4:18). Yet the emphasis for the modern Christian is not to be so heavily wealth-centred.

Abram was also promised **a great name**. Men and women generally wish to get a good name, and then they wish to maintain it. The thought of being totally nameless, totally ignored, totally insignificant to others is unbearably painful. In Genesis 3:20 Adam gave his wife a name, and in doing so he gave her significance. It meant that he was paying her attention, taking notice of her, and was seeing her place in the kingdom of God. In Genesis 4:17 Enoch, son of Cain, names a city after his own son. It was a means of being known for a long time and being treated as a notable person. In the third rebellion of the human race (after the first in Eden, and the second just before the flood) the troublemakers say *'Let us get ourselves a name'* (Genesis 11:4).

What men and women wish to get by ways of wickedness and self-confidence, God wishes to give them by grace – beginning with Abram! A great name!

It was the same with Jesus. When He was on planet earth He was disparagingly called 'Jesus of Nazareth'. *'He shall be called a Nazarene'* (Matthew 2:23). 'Jesus of Nazareth' is what they called Him when He was hanging on the cross (John 18:5). But by His obedience He was highly exalted and *'given a name'* that was above every name, so that at the name of Jesus – the despised name that His enemies used – every knee should bow and every tongue should confess that Jesus Christ is Lord! God gave Him a name (Philippians 2:5–11)!

It is the same with Christians. By God's choice our names are in the book of life before the foundation of the world. When we are converted we are in the same position as Abraham; there is the possibility that we shall be 'given a name'. If we overcome, Jesus will 'confess our name' before the Father (Revelation 3:5). Just as God glorifies His name, He will to a lesser extent glorify our name! An honoured position of recognition and authority is part of God's inheritance offered to Abraham and offered to us who are Abraham's children.

# Chapter 5

# Usefulness, Significance, Influence
(Genesis 12:2–3)

**Another assurance to Abram consists of the promise of usefulness to God**. God said, '...*and so you shall be a blessing'*. Abram will become a channel of blessing to others. The words are actually a command: 'And be a blessing!' It is a Hebrew way of making a very emphatic promise; it means '...and so you certainly shall be a blessing'.

Abram must respond to God in faith. If he persistently follows what God is saying to him, the child Isaac will be born, and from Isaac will come Jacob, and from Jacob will come the nation of Israel, and from the nation of Israel will come Jesus, and from Jesus will come every kind of blessing. We can become a blessing to others by being an example of faith. In Abram's case we see him taking God's word seriously, holding on despite mistakes, believing God when God's word to him seems quite impossible, trusting God's promises when circumstances seem to point in the opposite direction, overcoming the depression that comes when expectations are extremely delayed, refusing to be discouraged. Abram is a blessing by the sheer goodness of his example not as a super-saint but as one who persisted in believing no matter what!

We can become a blessing to others by contributing to the forward movement of God's kingdom. God had a plan for bringing salvation to the world. Abraham played a part in it – a big part. But we all have parts to play in carrying forward God's kingdom. Jesus must reign until He has put all enemies beneath His feet. But He reigns through us, through persistent believers.

We are children of Abraham! Be a blessing! Be a giant of faith! Trust God amidst delays and difficulties, discouragements and dangers, depressions and demons! And the promise to Abraham is ours too: 'you certainly shall be a blessing'.

**Another promise to Abram is what I might call the promise of significance**. The promise is that Abram will become so important in the plans of God that God will bless or curse according to how we relate to Him. '. . . *I will bless those who bless you . . . the one who curses you I will curse'* (12:3).

Abram is central in God's purpose to bring salvation. So anyone who resists what is happening in and through Abram is resisting God. Abram's faith is carrying forward God's programme of salvation.

Jesus said to his disciples: *'Anyone who receives you receives me, and anyone who receives me receives the one who sent me'* (Matthew 10:40). Anyone who is forwarding God's gospel, as Abram was and as Jesus' disciples were, is representing God. God will stand by him. When someone attacks God's servant, it is like attacking God. Equally when someone blesses one of God's servants because he is God's servant, then the one doing the blessing is himself blessed. He who receives a prophet because he is a prophet will receive a prophet's reward. He who receives Abram will receive Abram's reward. This is the blessing of Abraham. When we are people of faith, as Abraham was a man of faith, we gain the greatest significance conceivable. God stands by us. Woe to the person who curses us! What blessing there is for those who bless us because they receive what we have to say, what we are doing for God. *'Do not touch my anointed'*, says God, *'and do my prophets no harm'* (Psalm 106:15). God shows special displeasure at the ill-treatment of His servants, and special pleasure when His servants are honoured. Anyone who blesses God's servants are likely to find that they themselves are being blessed by God. When Abimelech threatened Abram and his seed he himself was threatened (Genesis 20); when he blessed Abram (20:16) Abimelech and his wife and his servants were themselves blessed through Abram's prayers (20:17–18). Something similar will be true in the lives of those who follow in the footsteps of Abram's faith.

**Abram was also promised influence among the nations**. God says: *'And in you all the families of the earth shall be blessed'*.

It has always been God's will that the blessings of salvation should come to all the world. There is only one God, and the human race is one in sin. God has one plan of salvation, and that one plan of salvation was coming into being through Abram. It was for all nations. Abram was not yet a Jew; he was not yet circumcised. He himself was simply a pagan from Ur. If he could be saved, anyone could be saved. Through the promise that Abram's seed was coming, there was blessing for anyone who accepted the promise. There was blessing immediately for anyone who had the same kind of faith as Abram had.

Five times in Genesis 1–11 the narrative uses the word 'curse' (Genesis 3:14, 17; 4:11; 5:29; 9:25). Five times the word 'bless' comes in Genesis 12:1–3. God's purpose to send a Saviour through Abram is God's answer to the curses falling upon the world through the three rebellions of Genesis 3:1–7, Genesis 6:1–8 and Genesis 11:1–9.

But the blessing ultimately would be in the person of Jesus. In Him there are treasures of wisdom and of knowledge. In Him is wisdom and righteousness and sanctification and redemption. Out of His fullness comes grace upon grace (see Colossians 2:3; 1 Corinthians 1:30; John 1:16).

These are the promises that are presented to Abram. God invites Abram to believe them and start travelling towards the promise land. *'So Abram left, as Yahweh had told him'* (Genesis 12:4). He responded in faith.

They are the same promises which belong to us. We too are promised some kind of territory to be occupied for God. We too shall experience multiplication, personal blessing, a name for faithfulness, usefulness to God, significance, international impact. 'Go forth', says God, 'and I will do it for you. By faith and patience, inherit the promises'.

# Chapter 6

## The Principles of Faith
(Genesis 12:4–9)

We have turned aside to consider the great promises to Abraham, but now we must come back to thinking about the nature of faith, as we see it in the story of Abraham.

We have seen (1) that faith is based on a revelation of God's will, and (2) that it is intensely personal. (3) Faith focuses especially on the promises of God. (4) Faith requires patience, and (5) faith and hope are closely linked. We have discovered (6) that faith may have to surmount great obstacles. Now there is more.

7. **Faith generates obedience**. *'So Abram left, as Yahweh had told him'*, says Genesis 12:4. It was a gigantic step for Abram. It certainly could not have been easy. He had to give up natural ties with his family and clan, and no doubt had to face a lot of disapproval, for a clan does not let go of one of its members easily. God said He would give Abram a land but at that time the Canaanites were there. God spoke of multiplying Abram so that he would become a nation, but at that time Sarai was barren. Many people would have resisted God's command, but Abram did not.

What led to his obedience was his faith. Faith pushes us into obedience. It is not violent; it does not force us. Yet it certainly puts powerful pressure on us. The more we believe God the easier it is to obey God. Obedience is natural to us if we are convinced that what God says is true and trustworthy. Faith is something powerful. It grips the heart. It is a deep persuasion that something we hear from God is true. We have to respond. It is as if we have no choice. When Abram heard these promises, he believed them. It was almost inevitable that

29

he should start travelling as God said. Faith generates obedience. *'Abram left, as Yahweh had told him'*.

8. **Faith is the opposite of sight**. God told Abram, *'Go forth ... to the land which I will show you...'*, but God did not say what land it was and Abram had never seen it. When Genesis 12:5 says they set out for Canaan the writer is speaking from a later viewpoint. It means that they were called to the place that, **as the writer knows**, turned out to be Canaan. Although Abram knew which direction to travel in, he did not know precisely where the land was until the point mentioned in Genesis 13:14–17. God leads us step by step. When you **see** something you no longer need faith. At Jesus' Second Coming, there will be no faith in Jesus because every eye shall **see** Him. If you are seeing it is not faith, it is seeing! Faith is believing now what everyone will believe one day. *'We walk by faith, not by sight'* (2 Corinthians 5:7).

9. **Faith includes involvement in practical matters**. Abram was not called to retire into a monastery or become a solitary hermit outside of ordinary society. Far from it! He travelled with Sarai his wife and took also his nephew Lot and a large community of workers and assistants plus many sheep and goats (12:5). Faith is not the opposite of practical skilfulness. Men and women of faith become practical in matters of everyday living. Faith is not super-religious! It is not like being alone in a cathedral; it is more like staying cool when you have a large and hectic family to care for. It is a matter of trusting God in the midst of earthly cares and responsibilities.

10. **Faith receives confirmations**. Abram had left Ur many years before with his family. Now he travels from Haran following the well-known western routes that travellers used. Eventually he gets to Shechem and the oak of Moreh. He finds the land is occupied by Canaanites (12:6). Then he receives a fresh encouragement. God appears to him (12:7). It is a confirmation that what he has been doing is right.

God does not like to give us 'signs' before we believe Him, but He likes to give confirmations after we believe Him. God had appeared to Abram before in Ur, but had not appeared to him for some time. When he gets to Canaan, God appears again. It was a confirmation of his faith. God likes us to believe Him whether He gives us special 'signs' or not, yet after we have trusted Him and have acted in faith He often lets something happen that rewards and confirms our faith.

Shechem was an ancient Canaanite town, roughly in the centre of the area that would later be known as Israel. It is at this point that God appears to Abram and gives him a fresh revelation.

11. **Faith leads to further understanding**. A new word appears in the story of Abram at this point: it is the word 'seed'. God says *'I will give this land to your seed'* (12:7). It is an eighth promise clarifying the seven promises of Genesis 12:2–3. The purpose of God will go forward through a 'seed'. The word 'seed', as we have noticed before (Genesis 3:15) is ambiguous. It can refer to a single entity, 'a seed'. It can be a collective word, 'seed' meaning many seeds. This means that the phrase 'seed of Abram' can be taken in more than one way. Actually there are four ways we can take it according to whether it is taken biologically or spiritually, collectively or singularly.

Biologically and as an individual, the seed is **Isaac**.

Biologically and as a group, the seed is **Israel** the earthly nation.

Spiritually and as an individual, the seed is **Jesus**.

Spiritually and as a group, the seed is **all believers** in Jesus.

At that moment Abram was probably thinking mainly of having a son and of the nation that would come through him, but God had more in mind than Abram realised. Yet his faith was growing in understanding. He was receiving fresh revelations from God. To him that has shall more be given.

## Chapter 7

# The Character of Faith
### (Genesis 12:4–9)

12. **Faith was sustained by worship and consecration**. In Abram's story we find him continually building altars for God. The first was at Shechem (12:7), then he built another between Bethel and Ai (12:8; see also 13:4). Then he built a third altar at Hebron (13:18). He was following the example of Noah who had also built an altar as soon as he was released from the ark (Genesis 8:20). Later on he would build one also at Moriah (22:9). Isaac built an altar at Beersheba (26:25), and Jacob would build a second altar at Shechem (33:20) and one at Bethel (35:1, 3, 7).

An altar was a place where a sacrifice was offered. Abram intended to use these places for times when he would offer sacrifices to God. He was continuing what had been begun by Abel. Abel pioneered the way of worshipping God by means of animal-sacrifice. The idea came from what God had done according to Genesis 3:24. God had killed an animal and covered the nakedness of Adam and Eve. By the death of an animal came a covering of their shame. Abel followed this hint from God. The death of an animal served as a sign that sin should be punished. The animal dies for the sins of the person offering the sacrifice. God accepted animal-sacrifice before Jesus came. The animal-sacrifice is a picture of what God will do through Jesus. The altars were places of faith in a substitutionary sacrifice. They were also places of prayer. Abram intended to have special times when he would seek God. We are to pray daily, but it is also good to have special times of prayer and days of prayer.

The altars were places of revelation. Often as Abram

trusted in God's sacrifice and looked for the presence of God in his life, God would speak to him. Then the altar would become a place of revelation.

The altars were places of consecration. The offering of the animal expressed the thought that a substitute was needed because the offerer was conscious of his imperfections. Yet it also expressed the desire that he himself should be wholly dedicated to God, 'burnt up' in the service of God.

By building these altars, Abram was expressing his conviction that the land would one day specially belong to God. He was turning the land into a place of worship already! And it expressed his intention to live by continued worship and consecration to God. Faith is not a dry, barren intellectualism. It is a matter of meeting God!

13. **Faith creates pilgrimage**. Abram had to keep travelling. He still needed further clarification as to precisely which parts of the land were to come to his seed. Explanation will come (see 13:14–17) but at the moment he is still exploring. He moves to the area east of Bethel, makes a camp between Bethel and Ai, and then builds a second altar (12:8) for fellowship with God. Then he closes down the camp and starts off on his travels again, moving further south. Faith creates pilgrimage. Abram was not being allowed to totally settle down and call Shechem or Bethel or Ai or Hebron his 'home'.

The Christian is a pilgrim, a traveller. It may not mean that we literally have to travel around, although that might be involved for some. But in spirit we are always to be pilgrims, travellers. We learn one lesson after another. We move on in the Lord's work from one stage to another.

Although Abram's first altar was in Shechem, an ancient town, the second one was not in a town but in the hills between two towns. Abram made his home a tent-encampment; it was a sign that he was not settling down with a large mansion in the nearest big town. He was a pilgrim and was not looking for great possessions in this world.

This is always to be the spirit and attitude with which we face life. God may give us a solid house! But in our attitudes we are always to have the spirit of a pilgrim, a nomad, a traveller. This world is not our home. Abram lived in something that was flimsy and temporary. We might well be given something better than that! But in spirit – and maybe quite literally – God calls us to know that we are here only temporarily.

It means that we must always be ready for a new calling from God. God's calling upon our lives will have unity in it, yet God's purpose is for us to 'evolve' and grow and develop. Each stage prepares for the next stage. Yet at any one point we must be ready to be called to move on to something that we have not been used to in the past. We are pilgrims not settlers!

It means that we must always be ready for upheaval. We are not to get too traditional and stuck in our ways. If our work for God and our ways of ministering for God are 100% identical to what we were doing ten years ago or even five years ago it is likely that we are not moving on with God. If we continue to do identically the same thing 'as it was in the beginning, is now and ever shall be' – it is likely that we are not open to new workings of God in our lives. We are (at least in spirit) to be like a traveller in a tent, not like a monarch in a mansion. It means that we must accept that life is facing one new thing after another – until we go to heaven.

# Chapter 8

## A Lapse of Faith
### (Genesis 12:10–20)

The life of faith is a life full of challenges. Almost as soon as he got to the land, he left it! Faith gets attacked. Sarah was barren (11:20); the land of Canaan is occupied (12:6). Now there comes another challenge. He had not been long in Canaan when the land was troubled by famine (12:10). When God calls us to a certain area of life, we must not be surprised if pressure comes which tends to move us out of what has been revealed as God's will. Abram had been called in this direction but suddenly it seems that Canaan is not a good place in which to stay.

1. **Abram falls into fear**. He faced a serious lack of food (12:10). What should we do if we lack vital provisions for ordinary health and livelihood? Abram was doing God's will, and was doing God's work, but suddenly there is a severe shortage of food.

He could stand firm and simply trust God. Or he could take practical steps to provide for himself, but if he is not careful this might open up the possibility of his stepping out of what God wants for him. This is in fact what happens. He steps out of God's will for his life. God had not called him to Egypt but to Canaan, and Abram had only just arrived in Canaan. But he is afraid.

2. **Abram acts prematurely**. He has not had much experience in Canaan yet, and is still young in this kind of life. In alarm he feels he must do something, and it seems that he will have to go to Egypt where there is likely to be more food. But it is premature.

3. **Abram falls into deceit**. Sarai was beautiful (12:11). Egyptians, politicians and kings liked to have plenty of women in a 'harem' – a household of wives, and Abram fears he might be killed (12:12). It is strange that he has boldly travelled to Canaan in the faith that he will be made into a great nation, but now he does not think he will be alive for more than a few weeks! Yet it is not so strange, since all Christians find it easier to trust in God for their eternal salvation than to keep trusting God when something alarming happens at this very moment!

He suggests she should pretend to be only his sister (12:13). It is half true, since Abram and Sarai had the same father but different mothers. Yet it is deceitful. It is also a case of self-centred and arrogant male supremacy – as was the universal norm in the ancient world. *'Say you are my sister so that it may go well with me!'*, says Abram. He is risking Sarai's safety and purity but that does not seem to worry him. It was a blind spot in his life, and typical of the world in which Abram lived, which treated all women badly. It is seen also in his polygamy, his treatment (and Sarai's treatment!) of female servants. Even Abram the father of believers was immature at this point.

4. **Abram ended up in a false position**. Sarai's beauty is noticed (12:14) and Abram has acted in a way that makes her more available to danger than if he had told the truth. She is taken into Pharaoh's house (12:15), and is on the way to being added to the number of Pharaoh's concubines. Abram does rather well out of it (12:16) and does not seem to be worrying about Sarai.

But it is terrible to be in a false position. It is dreadful to be in a position where your conscience is not clear and you feel you are not really being honest. It is awful to be in a place where you do not belong and living in a way that you know is not really right for you, and where you are claiming something that is not true.

Abram got himself into a false position because he was not open about his relationship to Sarai and to God.

However **God is faithful**. God stepped in, and was loyal to Abram. God is steadfast even when His servants fall into bad mistakes. God unmasked Abram. Since Abram would not extricate himself from his false position, God stepped in and did it for him, but it involved Abram's being exposed and disgraced. Abram was thrown out!

Pharaoh was afflicted with problems and reckoned his trouble was connected with Abram. Soon the truth came out (12:17–19) and Abram was sent away (12:20). There was nothing voluntary about it. Sometimes when we will not extricate ourselves from a compromising situation, God arranges to have us thrown out! God would prefer us to repent ourselves, but if we will not do so, He can arrange for us to be thrown out of a false situation somewhat violently. He does it for the sake of His purpose, because of His great determination to use us.

Abram made his way back to the area of Bethel (13:1–4). God had been good to him. He had not suffered as much as he might have done. God overruled in great mercy, and Abram and Sarai left Egypt unharmed.

After God had acted powerfully in this way Abram felt the need of forgiveness and restoration from God. So he went back to the place where he had sought God once before, and called on the name of Yahweh (13:4). Soon God would speak to him again (13:14).

We all know what it is to panic in a crisis and go through a lapse of faith. When we are young in Jesus it is understandable, but God wants us to recognize crisis for what it is – a testing of faith. If we lapse God will stand by us but there will be disgrace and pain. Better to continue believing and stand firm when faith is challenged.

# Chapter 9

## Greatness and Smallness

### (Genesis 13:1–13)

Abram has responded in faith to God's word. But, as we are seeing, there are various obstacles in the way of God's plan being fulfilled. Sarah is childless, the land is occupied, Abram is fallible. Now there arises a new emergency, a crisis in his relationship to Lot.

Abram has travelled from Egypt to the Negev, the dry area in the far south of Canaan (13:1). Abram is rich, and he and Lot have many herds of sheep and goats, and many employees who work for them (13:2). Abraham moves his flocks slowly towards the north, eventually reaching Bethel (13:3–4), where there is the altar he built earlier. After his misbehaviour in Egypt, he wants to go back to where he began and seek God.

Although God had told Abraham to leave his family (12:1), Lot also had faith in the promises to Abraham and so he had come with Abraham. God's word that Abraham should act in independence of his family had not been completely followed. Possibly Abraham was waiting for a suitable time. They soon found difficulty in having two small tribes so close together (13:5). Each group of herdsmen were struggling to make use of the same resources and the result was conflict (13:6). The grassland was over-grazed; the water was short. It led to strife (13:7), and to make matters worse the Canaanites were watching (13:7b)!

Abram responds with generosity; Lot seems to be rather greedy and self-centred. The life of faith involves learning to live with brothers and sisters, and Abram acts as a man of faith once again.

Consider **Abram's greatness**.

1. **It was Abram who suggested a friendly consultation** (13:8). Abram took the initiative. When there is some conflict with a brother or a person who is close to us in the Lord the question arises: who should take the initiative? The lazy, unbelieving way is to let the situation drift and get steadily worse. Abraham's way of faith involved boldly taking the initiative and acting to put things right.

2. **Abram made a friendly and practical appeal** (13:8). It was brotherly relationship which concerned him. 'We are brothers!', he said. The Canaanites were nearby and Abraham and Lot were representing God. The brotherhood that was between them meant a lot to Abraham. Faith involves taking brotherhood with other believers seriously.

3. **Abram recognized that sometimes friendly separation is the way of love**. When peaceful closeness has been proved to be impossible, it is sometimes right to maintain friendliness and love but allow freedom for each side to act separately (see Acts 15:39, and even 1 Corinthians 7:12–15).

4. **Abram acted with great generosity** (13:9). He says to Lot, 'Take what area seems the best to you. I will be quite happy with the remainder'. It is an act of great generosity and kindness. It is faith that enables Abraham to act in this way. A man of faith believes that God will care for him; he can afford to be generous.

Now consider **Lot's immaturity**.

1. **Lot was governed by sight rather than by faith**. Lot *'looked around'* (13:10). It was not God's promise that affected him but what he could see! The area down by the Dead Sea in the valley of the river Jordan was 'well watered'; that was the area he wanted! There was great beauty and fertility in the land close to the Dead Sea.

2. **Lot showed no generosity**. Although Abram was the older man, Lot showed little respect for him. He *'chose for himself'* (13:11) the best land he could find. There was no hint of any generosity to Abram. Large faith leads to generosity. Small faith leads to meanness.

3. **Lot was attracted by the nearby cities**. Not only did he move east into the Jordan valley; he also moves southwards

towards the cities at its southern tip. This is the second reference to cities in the Old Testament (see 4:17); they arose in the line of Cain. So far they have not seemed to be places of much blessing. Now in Genesis 13:12 their reputation is no better. Lot has little regard for spiritual danger. Lot now had the security of the big nearby town; we shall soon find him living in Sodom (19:1). But the men of that place were evil (13:13). Lot had no sense of avoiding spiritual danger.

Both Abram and Lot were believers in the promises. 2 Peter speaks of *'righteous Lot'*. Yet Abram was a man who applied his faith and worked it out in many areas. Lot was a man who failed to apply what he believed. He had faith in the promises to Abram and yet somehow this faith did not seem to affect his attitude to his kinsman or his attitude to wealth and riches.

The results of the two approaches to life showed in what happened to Abram. Abram is immediately blessed by God. He may have surrendered some territory for the sake of Lot, but immediately the incident was finished God spoke to Abram (Genesis 13:14–18) and gave him fresh assurance of the promises. There is no sign that God ever dealt very intimately with Lot in this way. Lot gained the world but almost lost his soul; Abram might seem to have lost something but he gained the presence of God as a reward.

As for Lot, he soon found that the wonderful territory near the south of the Dead Sea was not as secure as he thought it was. It seemed to him beautiful and well-watered but soon it was invaded by kings from the east. Eventually the area would be destroyed with fire and sulphur from heaven. Today the area of Sodom lies submerged under the waters of the southern end of the Dead Sea, 'well-watered' more than ever! Abram's bold generosity brought him blessing; Lot's meanness brought him nothing.

# Chapter 10

## Three Promises Repeated

(Genesis 13:14–18)

After his great generosity to Lot, Abram was rewarded by a fresh experience of God. Earlier, God's promise had first come to Abram in Ur (see 12:1–3). Then there came a clarification while Abram was in Shechem (12:7). Now for the third time God reaffirms what He is intending to do for Abram (13:14–17). The land of Canaan was full of altars for pagan gods. Abram has nothing to do with them; he is building his own altars for God. He is not on any multi-faith venture. He was in the programme of forwarding the kingdom of 'the God of Abraham', the God and Father of our Lord Jesus Christ.

There are three aspects to the promise being emphasized.

1. **Inheritance of the land**. The land has been mentioned before (12:1, 7), but now it is defined even more clearly. Abram is in the hill country near Bethel. From that high viewpoint he is invited to look as far as he can see. The entire land is for Abraham and his seed (13:14–15). Since Lot has also just been looking at a part of the land (13:10), it includes the area Abram has just allowed Lot to take for himself! God is offsetting what has just happened to Abram. Man's discouragement is followed by God's encouragement. Also the phrase 'for ever' or 'indefinitely' is added to the promise (13:15). The territory of Israel and all that it stands for is being given to Abraham and his seed for ever. God is able to keep giving us promises. When men and women discourage us, God is able to compensate for what they say and what they do by speaking to us again and reaffirming His intention for our lives.

In what sense was Abram himself given the land? He was

41

always a stranger and a pilgrim on planet earth (see Hebrews 11:10, 13–16). He was given the land partly in the sense that he was able to enjoy it. Christians are given the earth. I do not refer to worldly ownership. The promise has a spiritual meaning. We do not steal what belongs to others! We do not offend others by the way we use God's world. Yet the blessings of the world come to us. We inherit the earth – even now! All things are ours. Everything is organised by God so as to bless us. People bless us *'whether Paul or Apollos or Cephas'* (1 Corinthians 3:22). 'The world' is there to bless us. If we enjoy God, we enjoy everything! (1 Corinthians 3:22). Life blesses us. No matter what happens it will turn out for our good, if we are the called according to God's purpose.

Also the land was a foretaste of the future. In the sense of worldly ownership *'God gave him no inheritance ... not even a foot of ground'* (Acts 7:4).

2. **The quantity of 'the seed'**. The people are mentioned as well as the land. In Genesis 12:1–3, 7 it was clear that many people would be involved in God's promises. Now the number of Abraham's seed is spotlighted: it will be beyond counting, as much as the specks of dust throughout the earth (13:16). Abraham's seed will become an immense number.

Christians, the seed of Abraham, are part of a new people who will be overwhelming in their sheer quantity. We have not seen the end of the matter yet! When we finally see the 'great multitude' of people that have the same faith in God's promises as Abraham had we shall be delighted and astonished at the quantity of believers. The number will be staggering and is totally beyond our imagination, *'a great multitude, which no one could count'* (Revelation 7:9). Earthly citizenship is not eternally important. There will be no earthly citizenship in heaven. People may be proud of their nationality, their tribe, their surname, their culture-group, now, in this world. But in that day nothing of this nature will matter to us, except to be in the vast number of the saved.

3. **The presence of the future**. Abram is to start enjoying his inheritance by faith, even in his own lifetime! *'Arise, walk about the land ... I will give it to you ... '* (13:17). He starts to respond to this invitation to explore Canaan even further.

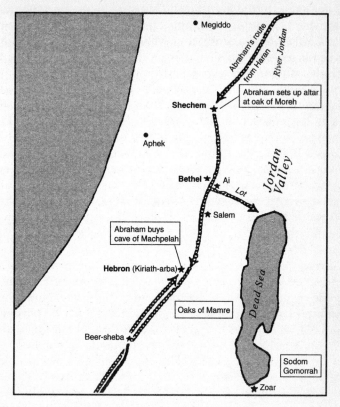

*Map 2   The towns of Abraham and Lot.*

Before this time his camps have been in the north, in Shechem, and in the central part of the land near Bethel. Now he moves further south, and makes his temporary home at Hebron (13:18). Abram's altar building continued. We have seen previous altars (Genesis 12:7, 8; 13:4). Now he builds one at Hebron (13:18). North, central, south – he was claiming the whole land for God.

It is to be noticed that the promise is *'to you and to your seed'*. It is for Abraham himself, and it is for Abraham's seed. In verse 17 the words are *'I will give it to you'*; Abraham's seed is not mentioned. It is typical of the Bible to tell us that we enjoy the future even now! This is what we can call 'the presence of the future'. Abram is to walk around the land of Israel and enjoy the prospect of what God is going to do. It is to be so real to him that it is as if he has the inheritance already. Although he has not strictly got everything God is going to give him, it is almost as if he has it already. *'Without receiving the promise'* (Hebrews 11:13) in the fullest sense, he sees it and embraces it and starts enjoying it (Hebrews 11:13). Abraham will be personally blessed by God. This has a lot to do with faith in the future. It is a matter of anticipating the future, in a way that is so real to us that it is like being in heaven before we are in heaven.

God says to each believer *'Arise, walk about the land ... I will give it to you ... '* (13:17).

# Chapter 11

## Four Kings Against Five
### (Genesis 14:1–16)

Abram has shown much faith (12:1–9), but alongside his faith there have been anxieties over his safety (12:10–20) and tussles in his relationship with Lot (13:1–13). But God has been faithful and His promises have been renewed and clarified (13:14–18). Now there comes a new crisis for Abram to handle.

In the days of Abram, round about 2000 BC, there came an occasion when four kings from Mesopotamia (mentioned in 14:1) declared war on five kings (mentioned in 14:2) who had territories at the southern end of the Dead Sea. These five city-states had been ruled by an Eastern king, Chedorlaomer king of Elam, for twelve years. Then they made an alliance (14:3) and in the thirteenth year they rebelled agaist Chedorlaomer (14:4). As a result war broke out; four kings against five.

The Eastern kings, led by Chedorlaomer invaded Canaan and conquered four tribes on the eastern side of the Dead Sea (14:6), continuing as far south as El-Paran. Then they turned towards the northwest conquering two further kingdoms in that southern area (14:7). At this point they were approaching the south of the Dead Sea and the five Canaanite kings went out to do battle; four kings aginst five (14:8–9). Lot was now living in the area of Sodom, so the warfare was being conducted in an area close to where he was living.

However the region south of the Dead Sea was full of bitumen pits, and when the battle went against the Canaanites and the kings of Sodom and Gomorrah fled with their troops, many men fell into these bitumen pits. ('They' in verse 10

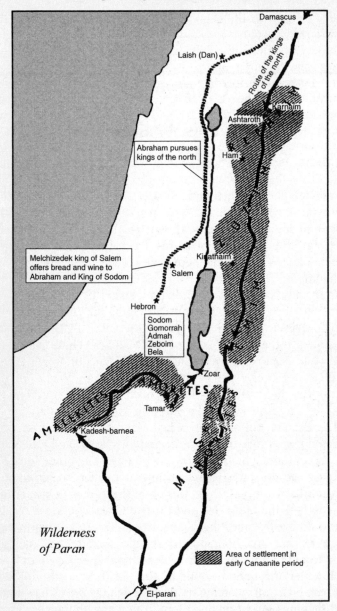

**Map 3** *Route of the kings who invaded Canaan.*

seems to refer to the soldiers rather than the kings.) Others fled to the hills (14:11).

Now Lot and Abram come into the story. The goods of the kings were captured, and so was Lot (14:11).

1. **Lot's unspirituality proves unprofitable** (14:12). We remember that when there had been a dispute over crowded land, Lot had been allowed to take the Jordan valley as his inheritance, leaving Abram with the higher territory that was more westerly. He himself has moved close to Sodom. It seemed to be a comfortable option that Lot had chosen, but now this is the very area south of the Dead Sea that had been invaded.

There are two ways of discovering that there is very little security in this world outside of God. There is the easy way and the hard way. The easy way is to believe God! God constantly warns us there is no security in earthly treasures. They can be lost overnight. War may smash our expectations. Everything deteriorates; 'moth and rust' can destroy. Thieves can break in and steal (Matthew 6:19). And if our treasures are not taken from us, we might be taken from our treasures, as the 'rich fool' of Luke 12:13–21 discovered.

If we believe God, we will be able to handle earthly treasures well, but if we will not learn the easy way there is a hard way, and that is to discover the insecurity of earthly treasures by bitter experience. Lot had to learn the hard way.

2. **The event is a challenge to Abram's peace** (14:13). He was living near Hebron in a place where there were many 'terebinths'. 'Terebinths' were trees that did not grow very high but their branches spread out and gave plenty of shade. Abram was living in a temporary home at a place called 'the Terebinths of Mamre'. He is in a friendly relationship with Mamre, Eschol and Aner, three nearby clan-leaders.

But if Abram ever imagined he was going to be left to live a leisurely life in the countryside under the shade of the trees, he soon found that it was not to be! A messenger arrives; Lot has been taken prisoner.

There is no permanent easy peace for the believer. It is true that there is God's peace, but God's peace is not an easy life. It is rather an assurance of being reconciled to Him and having Him as ally and friend in every trouble. In a worldly sense God brings 'not peace but a sword'. We may have peace within, peace with God, but there is no promise of soft and easy living.

3. **The event is a challenge to Abram's generosity** (14:13). What did Abram feel, we wonder, when the news first came to him about Lot? It would be easy to say 'It serves him right!'. Yet Abram felt obliged to help (14:13). If he felt any resentment against Lot he does not let it trouble him for long. He acts with speed, and takes time, effort and energy, and uses all his resources to rescue his nephew Lot (14:14–16). He is showing generosity to a brother-believer who has badly treated him!

Paul tells us that if it is possible we must live at peace with everyone. Sometimes it is not possible. Abram was not finding his nearby chiefs and rulers to be very peaceable. But, says Paul, we are not to take revenge. In many situations where we are ill-treated we are to do nothing, and God will act. When Lot was dealing rather unfairly with Abram, Abram did nothing. Lot treated him badly, but Abram simply let him have his way. 'Leave room for the wrath of God', says Paul. Often when we are ill-treated we are tempted to act vengefully. Abram did nothing. Soon God acted and Lot learnt that there was no security in greed.

Abram was not being overcome by Lot's evil ways; he was overcoming evil with good. We have to get to the point where we are actually obeying Romans 12:17–21. It is easy to admire the idea of overcoming evil with good. Abram is not simply admiring the idea; it is the way he has learned to live.

# Chapter 12

## Melchizedek

(Genesis 14:17–24)

Abram had entered into danger and hardship in order to rescue Lot. Now as he returns he is weary and troubled, but God has a way of encouraging him.

1. **Abram meets a unique high-priest of God** (14:17–18). Melchizedek was king in Salem, the town which would later be known as Jerusalem. Evidently the knowledge of the true God was present in Salem; perhaps the truth about God had been passed down from the days of Noah. This king had been appointed to represent Him in the city-state of Salem, and Abraham regarded him as his spiritual superior.

The 'order' of his priesthood was unique. He did not get his priesthood by inheriting it. Unlike every other spiritual leader mentioned in Genesis, no genealogical record is given. He is *'without father, without mother'* (Hebrews 7:3) in the book of Genesis (but not without parents altogether!).

'Salem' means 'peace'. His own name, Melchi-zedek, means 'king of righteousness'. So he was 'king of Peace', in that he ruled in a city known for peace, and he was 'king of righteousness' in his own person. He combined righteousness and peace in his people and in his own person.

We can see why the New Testament says that Jesus is a great high-priest *'after the order of Melchizedek'*. Like Melchizedek, Jesus is king of peace and king of righteousness at the same time. Like Melchizedek, Jesus is a not a high-priest by inheritance, but is a unique high-priest without precedent or successor.

Abram finds encouragement in meeting such a person as Melchizedek. After some heavy conflict and as he is returning from battle, Melchizedek comes out to meet him. It is a perfect picture of how Jesus comes to our aid and our rescue when we need Him. After periods of conflict and testing, Jesus Himself has a habit of coming to visit us. He brings encouragements and talks to us of the things of God. Jesus is our sympathetic high-priest in a unique 'order'; there is no one like Him.

2. **Abram is refreshed with bread and wine**. Melchizedek knows that Abram has been in a battle to rescue a wayward nephew. He knows that Abram will be hungry and tired. So he comes out to meet him bringing bread to build up his strength, and diluted wine, several parts water, one part wine, to refresh him and give him energy again. It was obviously not the 'strong drink' against which we have warnings in the book of Proverbs.

When Jesus comes to meet us He brings us bread. He Himself is the bread of life. We feed on Him; we 'eat' Him. It means that we trust Him. Every part of His life and ministry is for us. We take hold of Him like a hungry man grasping food.

Jesus is wine to us. He refreshes us. He comes to us full of goodness and sweetness, full of promises. We are refreshed when He manifests Himself to us and imparts His gifts to us.

3. **Abram is prayed for by Melchizedek** 14:19. *'Blessed be ... '* means 'I am praying for you to be blessed by God'. God had promised Abraham, 'I will bless you', but now the blessing comes through a unique high-priest from a unique city called 'Peace'. Like Melchizedek, Jesus ever lives to make intercession for us. He presents His requests for us to the Father. It is not that He is begging or pleading, but He definitely has requests for us. He prays without ceasing; He never has to sleep as the priests of the tribe of Aaron did. He never retires as the levitical priests had to retire. He never dies. He never makes a mistake. He prays with perfect faith and with perfect sympathy. The Christian lives on the intercession of Jesus.

4. **Melchizedek points Abram to God's greatness when he uses the words 'God Most High'**. This is the name that the people of Salem use for God. They do not speak of El Shaddai or Yahweh; their name for God is 'El Elyon'. It is a

compound name which uses the word 'El' ('God') but has another word to describe God. It is used three times in Genesis 14:18, 19, 20 and a fourth time with Yahweh, 'Yahweh God Most High', in 14:22. 'El Elyon' can be translated 'God Most High'. Melchizedek and his people were conscious that there were other spiritual beings that claimed to be 'gods' or 'sons of the gods'. They are not 'God' in the full sense of the term but there are angels and evil spirits which have an invisible spiritual nature and are sometimes called 'gods'. 'El Elyon', 'God Most High', expressed the thought that the God of Melchizedek is the one and only God above all other claimants to deity. The idea of being 'above' also expresses the notion of control. The God of Melchizedek is the Lord; He is 'over' everything.

5. **Melchizedek receives Abram's tithes** (14:20b–23). Abram has been wrestling with anxieties about possessions ever since he surrendered the best choice of the land to Lot. Now there is a further anxiety since he will refuse to get financial and material gain from the king of such a wicked place as Sodom (14:21–24). Yet his anxiety about prosperity does not stop him from tithing. He gives a tenth of what he has gained to Melchizedek. What made Abraham do this? It was not the Mosaic law. It did not yet exist. Abraham was being led by the Spirit. When we are led by the Spirit we shall fulfil the law even if it does not exist! The Christian will tithe and more-than-tithe if he is led by the Spirit.

6. **Abram's appreciation for God is enlarged**. He now uses the term *'Yahweh, God Most High'*. Abram knows that 'Yahweh' (a word he uses for God) and 'El Elyon', 'God Most High', are one and the same. Abram speaks of 'Yahweh' and Melchizedek speaks of 'El Elyon', but then Abram uses the phrase *'Yahweh, God Most High'* (Genesis 14:22). He brings the two names together! His experience of the priestly ministry of Melchizedek has led him into a greater understanding of God.

# Chapter 13

## Doubt and Assurance

(Genesis 15:1–6)

1. **Men and women of faith may face attacks of doubt**. Abram received great encouragements from God, yet he still could have doubts. He soon received the answer to Melchizedek's praying. Genesis 15:1 is a link with chapter 14. There have been anxieties about security and about possessions, and doubts about the promises which seem incredibly slow in coming to fulfilment. He has experienced a minor tribal war in which he has been in danger and was risking losing what material possessions he had. Melchizedek has prayed for him. What happens in Genesis 15:1 is surely the answer to Melchizedek's praying. God appears to him and reassures him at the very two points where he needs reassurance. 'I am your shield', says God; Abraham has just been in a war. 'Your reward, your wages shall be very great'. The word is the one normally used for salary or wages. Abram has just been anxious about material possessions. God answers that anxiety too.

Yet even great men of faith can find their trust in God attacked by doubts, and immediately after the reassurance Abram is in uncertainty. God sometimes seems to take a long time to fulfil His promises and we get discouraged. God had given wonderful promises to Abram, and yet they seemed so slow in coming. Now Abram has problems (15:2). *'O sovereign Yahweh'*, he says, *'what will you give me?'* God has for a long time been promising that he will become a great nation, but he cannot even have his first child! *'The heir of my house is a man of Damascus, Eliezar'*. Could it be, Abram wonders, that the 'seed' God will give him is to be someone he

52

adopts? 'Exactly what is it you are going to give me?' he asks God. When fulfilment of God's promises is delayed we think of lesser possibilities and are tempted to be content with less than God wants to give us. He is willing to accept a servant as an adopted son (15:2–3). He will accept anything if only God starts fulfilling His promise to give him a seed. But actually in suggesting the possibility that Eliezar might be the heir Abram is accepting less than what God wants to give him.

2. **God knows how to renew His promise**. At a time when Abram is perplexed and is tempted to accept less than what God has in mind, God comes with a fresh revelation. Eliezar is not the seed. It is from Abram's own body that the promised seed will come.

This is now the fourth time the promise has been given. First they were given in Ur (12:1–3), then in Shechem (12:7). God gave him promises a third time after Lot had separated from him (13:14–17). This is now a fourth occasion when God tells Abram of His plans (15:4–5).

God knows just how much we can stand. Abram is almost at breaking point and is ready to burst out with a cry of perplexity even at the very time when God is giving him a double assurance of protection and provision. So God comes to his aid with even more confirmations of His promises.

3. Not only does God renew His promise. **God progressively enlarges the promise as we walk in fellowship with Him**. God gives more information about how the heir will come to Abram. It will not be a matter of adopting a servant; Abram's son and heir will be fathered by Abram himself (15:4). Also the emphasis on numbers is now intensified. Abram is taken outside and asked to count the stars. He cannot do it. *'So shall your seed be'*, says God (15:5).

God follows these procedures of delaying His promise almost unbearably, because it is necessary. Somehow God's delays refine us and drive us to have further dealings with God and to seek personal contact with Him. If the promises of God flowed into our lives with ease and without our seeking them, we would forget where they come from.

4. **True faith is not altogether lost**. The fresh word from God reactivates Abram's faith. God's word is enough for Abram.

His response to what God says is immediately reasserted. *'Abram believed Yahweh and it was reckoned to him for righteousness'*. It is a mistake to think that Abram was justified at precisely this point. It is not that Abram is **first** approved by God at this point. Abram's faith had begun in Ur, and faith in God's word concerning the promised salvation was saving the very first time God's word came to Abram. He must be regarded as having been justified even in Ur, and certainly in Haran. The statement in Genesis 15:6 lets us know that again Abram responds to God. It does not mean that Abram believed God for the first time; that would totally contradict Genesis 12–14.

We are told what this persistent, triumphant, faith did for Abram. Abram's faith brought him a covering of God's righteousness. True faith rises above doubt. At this point Abram showed that the faith he had had for a long time, was true, lasting, permanent trust in God. It was the kind of faith that rose above doubts. Abram's faith had **always** brought him justifying righteousness – so had Abel's faith, and Enoch's faith, and Noah's faith – but this is an appropriate point to mention how faith in God's promise *'is reckoned for righteousness'*. Abram's faith rises above doubt. Saving faith is assurance about God's promise. Abram has had this kind of faith ever since the time of Genesis 12:4 if not even earlier. But it is appropriate that at **this** point the covering righteousness of God should be mentioned because Abram has shown quite clearly that his faith is saving assurance in God's word of promise, and is a faith that persists and recovers when doubts attack.

# Chapter 14

## Justification By Faith
### (Genesis 15:6)

Genesis 15:6 is one of the great statements of the Bible. It is quoted by Paul (Romans 4:3, 9, 22; Galatians 3:6) and by James (James 2:23). It is the heart of a good relationship with God, and the starting point of every blessing of the life of faith.

1. **Salvation starts with being given a covering righteousness**. *'Abram believed Yahweh and that was reckoned to him for righteousness'* (15:6). This is the heart of the gospel. Our problem is that we are sinners by birth, sinners by nature, sinners by routine. Nothing we can do can cancel out this sinful status, sinful habit, sinful character, sinful record. Amendment is not good enough; it cannot wipe out the past nor is our self-betterment ever totally successful. What we need is a covering. We need to be declared righteous before God even though in ourselves we are weak and wayward. This is precisely what we are given when we believe God's promise concerning salvation, concerning Jesus or (as Abram would have put it) concerning 'Abram's seed'. It was this that Paul made much of. He spoke of *'a righteousness that is by faith'* (Romans 1:17). Salvation starts when God gives us a gift of righteousness which is not at all ours but which comes wholly from God.

2. **God's protecting righteousness is 'reckoned' to us and is not produced by us**. It is very important to grasp this word 'reckoned'. A lot of people seem to have the idea that we save ourselves with the help of God's grace, but if we grasp hold of this word 'reckoned' we shall see that it is not our character either before we are saved or after we are saved, that enables us

to stand before God. It is not **our** character or behaviour at all. It is God's righteousness, God's holy character being attributed to us long before He ever works any changes in us. And even after God does work some changes in our character it is not those changes that enable us to stand acceptable before God. We are always, always, always, able to stand before God only because of a righteousness which He 'reckons' as ours.

3. **It is faith alone that brings a covering righteousness.** *'Abram believed Yahweh and that'* – his believing and nothing else – *'was reckoned to him for righteousness'*.

4. **This being 'reckoned' righteous is not the result of godliness.** Actually there is every reason to believe that Abraham was a complete pagan when God first called him. Abraham's family worshipped other gods but God summoned Abraham out of the darkness of Mesopotamian paganism. Genesis contains no mention of any special obedience on Abraham's part that led to his being reckoned righteous. It does not say 'Abram **obeyed** Yahweh and that was reckoned to him for righteousness'; it says *'Abram **believed** Yahweh and that was reckoned to him for righteousness'*. It was his faith that brought him a 'reckoned' righteousness; it was not his obedience that saved him.

5. **This being 'reckoned' righteous did not involve the Mosaic law.** Actually the Mosaic law did not exist! This is Paul's point in Galatians 3:15–18. The law came into Israel's history four centuries after Abram was 'declared righteous'. How could obedience to the Mosaic law be necessary if the Mosaic law did not exist when Abraham was 'justified'?

6. **This being 'reckoned' righteous did not involve circumcision of Israelite nationality**. This is Paul's point in Romans 4:9–10. Abram was credited with righteousness before he was circumcised. Paul's argument in Romans 4:9–10 can be applied to other signs and ceremonies. Abram was justified without being circumcised. He was also justified without being baptized, without being confirmed, without the Lord's Supper, without going to 'Mass'. If any of these signs and ceremonies were necessary for salvation, Abram could not have been the model of salvation since he had none of them at the time he was justified. But Abraham is the model of

salvation, the father of all believers. Our passage does not say 'Abram was circumcised and that was reckoned to him for righteousness'. It does not say 'Abram was baptized and that was reckoned to him for righteousness'. None of these things are involved in our justification. Abraham is the model! And only faith is mentioned as the channel by which God's righteousness is reckoned as being ours. Faith alone without work brings a covering righteousness. Faith alone without ceremony brings a covering righteousness. Faith alone without Jewish nationality brings a covering righteousness.

7. **What then is faith? It is assurance about God's word of promise**. It is not an assurance about oneself, but it is an assurance about God and His word. Abraham is quite unsure about himself but whenever God speaks he is sure that what God says is true and right, and he is able to build his whole future on the truth of what God has said.

We have 'faith' when we boldly believe in 'Abraham's seed', Jesus. We have 'faith' when we boldly take God at His word, believing that we are righteous before God although we are sinful in ourselves. We are righteous before God through a Person, through Abram's seed. Abram himself had a shadowy preview, but now we are able to spell it out in fullness and explicitly. The righteousness that is given to us is the righteousness of Jesus. As soon as we trust Abraham's seed, Jesus, we are given the covering righteousness of Jesus' holy obedience. God sees us as if we were as holy as Jesus! We are 'reckoned' to be as righteous as He is. It is true for us, the very second we take Jesus as our Saviour. When we believe in Jesus, our believing links us to Jesus and His righteousness is reckoned as ours.

# Chapter 15

## Driving the Vultures Away
### (Genesis 15:7–11)

Abram had expressed his anxiety (Genesis 15:2,3), and so God began making a covenant with Abram to help him. We have come across 'covenant' before in Genesis. A **'covenant' is a promise which has an oath added to it**.

**There are three kinds of covenant**: covenants of obligation to a senior, covenants of generosity towards a junior, and two-way covenants between equals. In Genesis we have seen the 'covenant of generosity' for the world through Noah (6:18; 9:19, 11, 12, 13, 15, 16, 17) and now we have another 'covenant of generosity' which God makes for Abraham's seed through Abraham (see Genesis 15:18; 17:2, 4, 7, 7, 9, 10, 11, 13, 13, 14, 19, 19, 21, where the word 'covenant' is used).

Noah's covenant was a covenant of generosity. We saw once before some of its ingredients. (i) It has a promise. (ii) It has an oath; it is a promise with an oath added to it. (iii) A covenant of generosity has a beneficiary, someone who is receiving the blessing of the oath. (A different kind of covenant, a covenant of law, has a 'victim', a target, a person who is obliged to swear allegiance.) (iv) A covenant of generosity is unconditional, after it has been given, although (v) it might be given as a reward. (vi) A covenant may take time to take place because it is not settled until the oath is given. (vii) A covenant may have attached to it a sign or symbol of some kind. (viii) A covenant involved the shedding of blood in some kind of sacrifice.

Now we take a closer look at these matters, in connection with this covenant with Abram.

In a nutshell the teaching is this. A **covenant is a bond or**

**relationship with God**. Christians are in 'covenant' with God. Christians have to get to a level of obedient faith so that God takes an oath to them personally. The covenant to Abram has already been made, so their salvation is secure. 'Abraham's seed' will not be lost. Yet our own 'oath of God's mercy' must be personally sought from God. When God swears in His mercy then our calling will be achieved, the Christian 'enters into rest' with regard to that particular matter. However I am jumping ahead! Let us come back to Abram and see how this matter works out in his life.

In the case of Abram:

1. **the covenant began with a reminder**. Genesis 15:7 tells Abram what God has done for him (*'I brought you out...'*) and what the purpose of his salvation is (*'...to give you this land to possess it'*). The word 'possess' is linked with the Hebrew word for 'inheritance'. It means 'possess as an inheritance'.

The purpose of salvation is inheritance. God brought us out in order to bring us in. We were brought out of idolatry in order to be brought into our inheritance. Inheritance is not salvation, but it is what initial salvation is leading towards.

2. **The covenant has a promise in it**. Verse 7b reminds Abram of the promises. 'This is what I want to do for you', says God. 'I am wanting to fulfil these promises in your life. I am wanting you to achieve an inheritance in this land of Canaan'.

3. **Covenant is designed to encourage and to motivate**. Abram has doubts (15:8). Although he has been given the promises several times (12:1–3, 7; 13:14–17), Abram still has doubts. It seems such an immense thing to believe. There is not much indication that anything that he has been promised is actually happening. Abram often wonders whether he has misunderstood.

So here he asks 'O sovereign Yahweh, how may I **know** that I shall possess it?'. He is unsure. 'How may I know?' he asks. In reply God starts a covenant-making procedure. **Covenant-on-offer is God's encouragement and God's motivation to believers who might be overwhelmed by doubts**.

I think it is important to realise that the covenant is only 'on offer' at this point. As the story of Abraham develops it will become clear that the oath is not actually given until Genesis 22:16 when God says *'By myself I have sworn'*. At the moment God is offering an oath, but the actual swearing of the oath does not come until later.

4. **The covenant begins with blood-sacrifice**. Five animals are brought and are killed (Genesis 15:9–10). They are the same five 'clean' animals that are used in the later sacrificial system in the law of Moses. Covenant always has the shedding of blood as its starting-point. This was the custom of the ancient world, but it also has importance in the gospel of Jesus. It looked forward to Jesus. The death of Jesus on the cross for our sins is the starting point of any relationship with God. One cannot even begin to be in relationship with God unless sin is atoned for in some way. So in the ancient world, the shedding of blood came in at an early stage in the procedure of any covenant.

5. **The one receiving the promises has to protect the blood-sacrifice**. Two rows of partly sacrificed animals are laying there in the open countryside. In the evening Abram will be given a revelation and will learn more of what God is promising to do for him, but for the moment the pieces of the sacrifice are laying there exposed. Not surprisingly vultures are swooping down from the sky seeking to snatch up the pieces of the sacrificed animals. It is a familiar sight to anyone who has travelled in tropical countries. Abram stays there driving away the birds of prey that are swooping down from the sky seeking to seize pieces of meat. Eventually God will speak to him but while he is waiting he must protect the blood sacrifice.

The basis of everything that will come to Abram is the shedding of blood and he must not let anything damage or spoil the sacrifice that God has provided. Something like this is involved in the Christian life. The basis of every blessing we receive is the blood of Jesus Christ. Vultures will swoop down from the sky to detract from the cross of Jesus. Some preachers will stress some particular favourite doctrine and soon you have a semi-cult with no atonement in its preaching. Paul said *'God forbid that I should glory in anything except in the cross of our Lord Jesus Christ'*.

There is the vulture of scepticism and religiosity. Many religious people do not seem to realise that the basis of Christian faith is the cross of Jesus. Sometimes they are offended about talk of Jesus' atonement. But the sacrifice of Jesus is crucial; the vultures must be driven away. Without the blood of Jesus there will be no inheritance, no experiencing of the promised blessings of God.

# Chapter 16

## Covenant and Oath
### (Genesis 15:12-21)

Covenant-relationship is oath-on-offer. When God is in covenant with someone or with a group of people, it means that He is making or is about to make an oath. Every Christian is in covenant-relationship with God through the blood of Jesus. God is offering to make an oath to every Christian. He is willing to say to every Christian 'Now I know that you fear me; I will indeed bless you'.

In Genesis 15–22 one covenant is spread over a number of chapters. The promise first came in Genesis 12. There is no totally **new** promise in Genesis 15. Genesis 15 is the start of a covenant, but there is no covenant sign and no verbal oath. The covenant-sign comes in Genesis 17; the covenant oath is finally given (after Abram has reached a high level of obedience) in Genesis 22. No oath-language is found in anything said to Abram before Genesis 22:16–17.

God was offering to give Abram an oath. He was getting ready to say 'I swear by myself ... I will surely bless you'. When God gives an oath He 'makes up His mind' to do that which He has been promising. The promise can never be lost once God has given an oath.

This subject can be studied in connection with God's oath to Noah,[1] or in connection with God's oath to David.[2] Further aspects of covenant-and-oath can be seen in Genesis 15:12–21. We have seen (1) the covenant began with a reminder; (2) the covenant has a promise in it; (3) covenant is designed to motivate; (4) the covenant begins with blood-sacrifice; (5) the one receiving the promises has to protect the blood-sacrifice. We continue.

6. **The burden of fulfilling the covenant is God's**. God puts Abram into a deep sleep. It reminds us of Genesis 2:21. God put Adam to sleep before giving him Eve. It was a way of making it clear that Eve came to Adam without Adam's efforts, and wholly by God's working. Adam was not a participant in creating Eve. The story in Genesis 15:12 is similar. It lets us know that the promise is entirely God's and it is His responsibility to bring it to pass. It is far from being Abram's plan. He is asleep when God announces it to him! Abram only has to follow God's lead. The burden of fulfilling the covenant will be the Lord's. The 'thick and dreadful darkness' is a theophany, a representation of the presence of God comparable to that in Exodus 14:20, Deuteronomy 4:11, 5:22, 23, 1 Kings 8:12 and 2 Chronicles 6:1.

7. **The covenant has predictive prophecy in it**. In Genesis 15:13–16, Abram is given a predictive outline of Israel's future history. When God is about to act He generally gives some kind of preview of what is about to happen. Prophets are often fore-tellers. God does nothing without revealing His plan to prophets (see Amos 3:7). Deuteronomy 18:9–10 warned that Canaanites have their demon-possessed men who seek to predict the future by the powers of evil spirits. Over and against such people God gives a prophet who accurately predicts what God will do (Deuteronomy 18:22). Men like Elisha often knew the future (2 Kings 6:12). Ezekiel knew Jerusalem well without ever going there (Ezekiel chapters 8–11). The prophets sometimes even knew the precise names of men who would be involved in God's kingdom centuries before those men appeared (1 Kings 13:2; Isaiah 44:28; see also Acts 9:12). Moses went to the king of Egypt knowing in advance what would happen (Exodus 3:19–25). Jesus' coming as a Jew, from the tribe of Judah, in the line of David, born of a virgin in the town of Bethlehem was all predicted before it happened. And every Christian knows in advance that Jesus will come in glory and majesty and every eye will see Him. All the mighty plans of God are revealed before they happen.

Even with individuals, we can expect to have a preview of how God is going to use us. At his conversion Saul of Tarsus knew what his work would be and who he would preach to (Acts 22:21); and he knew what would happen in the next few days as well (Acts 22:17–18)! I myself, as a teenager preparing myself to be a scientist, was gripped with the conviction that I would spend my life preaching instead! A few years later I had a strong feeling that the location of my work would be Kenya. It took Paul ten years to get to the Gentiles (Acts 13:2–3 was ten years after his conversion). I was brought by God to Kenya 13 years after my conviction that I would fulfil my calling there – and in a most unexpected manner. And a year before I went there, when passing one day through Nairobi, God gave me a powerful revelation that I would live near Argwings Khodek road. The anticipation was fulfilled. One year later I came to Nairobi; without any manipulation on my part. I lived near Argwings Khodek road. Eventually I moved away from that precise location, but I still drive up and down it almost every day. I was shown the very road a year before I moved to Nairobi!

Predictions large and small are built into God's ways of doing things. Abram is told that his descendants would go to a foreign country (15:13) and would be enslaved there (15:13). Years later, through Joseph, it happened. Abram was told that they would be delivered from bondage (15:14). Centuries later it happened; Israel was rescued from Egypt. Abram was told about his own personal future (15:15). The approximate timing of the events was given to him (15:16).

8. **God offers an oath if Abram will persistently believe**. In Genesis 15:17, God (represented by a flame blazing in a fire-pot) passes through the pieces of sacrificed animals. Although it is difficult to interpret, it is almost certainly God's way of representing an oath. He is speaking in visual symbolic form of the fact that one day He will take an oath. There is no oath yet; it comes in 22:16–17. But God represents what He will do. The passing between the animals is an ancient covenant-ceremony. It is God's way of saying 'May I be cut to pieces like these animals if I do not keep my promise'. It is similar to the ceremony mentioned in Jeremiah 34:18. God is offering Abram an oath. It has not come yet, but it is being offered.

9. **The promise gets expanded**. Genesis 15:18–21 is roughly

the same as the promises that have been given before, but God gives greater detail. It is still a promise, not an oath.

10. **The beneficiaries are Abram's seed** (15:18). All who may be called 'Abram's seed' will get the fulfilment of the promise – once the oath of Genesis 22:16–17 is finally given.

We shall see the outworking of this matter in the remaining stories of Abram's life. The full consummation and the giving of the oath will come when Abram has reached a certain level of obedience (22:1–18). Soon (Genesis 17:1–27) we shall be introduced to the covenant sign, circumcision.

The new covenant is parallel at every point. (i) The covenant has a promise. The promise is the blessings of the Holy Spirit. (ii) Every Christian is in a relationship where God is offering to take an oath about His promised blessings. In Hebrews it is called 'entering into rest'. (iii) The beneficiaries are believers and their seed on condition that they are saved (Acts 2:39). (iv) The blood of the covenant is the blood of Jesus Christ. (v) When God swears to us, the promise concerned will not thereafter be lost. (vi) It takes time to enter rest. (vii) The covenant-signs are baptism and the Lord's Supper. (viii) It takes effect by our depending on the blood of Jesus Christ.

## Footnotes

[1] See my *Genesis 1–11* (Sovereign World, 1996) chapters 7, 30, 32.

[2] See my *2 Samuel* (Sovereign World, 1996), chapters 12–13, and the story of David after 2 Samuel 7. See also my *Theology of Encouragement* (Paternoster, 1995), pp.62–66, 176.

# Chapter 17

# Running Ahead of God
### (Genesis 16:1–16)

For a long time Sarai had been unable to have a child, and so now Abram overwhelmed by doubts and perplexities, is doubting whether the promised 'seed' will ever be born through Sarai. Everyone in Genesis 16 acts badly. Only God stands out well.

1. Consider first, **the confusion of the three characters in the story** (16:1–4).

Sarai was feeling a failure. She had never been able to bear a child (16:1), and in most cultures a childless woman experiences a lot of suffering. Everything God had promised had been for Abram. Abram even spoke of adopting a servant as his son and heir (15:2). He seemed to have given up hope for Sarai. And God seemed to be against her. *'Yahweh has prevented me from bearing children'* (16:2).

Shame, guilt, a poor self-image, lack of confidence – they all tend to produce confusion and blunders. Sarah had an Egyptian servant-girl, Hagar, who had been with her since the trip to Egypt (12:10–20). Abram had been told that 'the seed' was to come from his own body (15:4). In those days, it was possible for a man with a childless wife to make use of a slave-girl in order to produce a child. In such a situation the childless wife took the child as her own and the true mother had no rights in the matter. So Sarai suggests that the pagan custom be followed and that Abram should get a child through Hagar.

She was acting without sense, without foresight, without guidance, without assurance. She could only say *'it may be'* (16:2).

Abram made mistakes as well. He *'listened to the voice of Sarai'* (16:2). Previously he had got his guidance from God; now he was getting his guidance from his wife. Adam had done the same (Genesis 3:6). A wife's counsel can be useful (see Judges 13:23) but it is not to be followed without thought.

Rather than persist in faith, Abram was turning to 'the flesh' (as Paul put it in Galatians 4:23). Rather than exercise patience he was acting prematurely. It seemed that God was not going to do anything special to produce the seed and Abram felt that he had to do something himself.

Hagar had been a slave-girl for many years. To sleep with Abram meant that she was being taken as a subordinate wife (16:3). For a slave-girl it was a kind of 'promotion'! Abram takes Hagar in the way that Sarai had suggested (16:4). She becomes pregnant. But then she starts acting with scorn towards Sarai. Apparently she thinks that she has now replaced Sarai as the one through whom Abram's expectations will be fulfilled.

2. **Running ahead of God brings trouble for everyone involved**. It all leads to bitterness. Sarai resents the way that she is being treated.

It leads to Sarai's blaming someone else. She blames Abram – although it was her idea in the first place! Abram is no doubt eagerly awaiting the birth of his son (but what if it had been a daughter?) and thinks that the son to be born of Hagar is the promised seed. It is not himself, Sarai and her future son Isaac that he has on his mind, but himself, Hagar and Ishmael! It is inevitable that, if he thinks Ishmael is the promised seed, he must be thinking of Hagar as the honoured mother of the chosen line. The idea that the child will belong to Sarai (16:2) is not totally realistic. Sarai has been displaced. Sarai is furiously resentful, and is ready to call God's judgement down upon her husband. *'May Yahweh judge between you and me'* (16:5).

It leads to further irresponsibility on the part of Abram. *'Do to her what you like'* (16:6), he says. Yet this leads to suffering for Hagar. He refuses to be involved in the matter at all – but this is irresponsibility.

It leads to cruelty by Sarai and suffering for Hagar. Sarai

treats Hagar harshly and Hagar runs away heading for Egypt (16:6b).

3. **Where sin abounds, grace abounds all the more**. God shows mercy when everyone else is showing their foolishness.

It was mercy when God sought Hagar (16:7). The 'angel of Yahweh' is God Himself, appearing in visible form. *'No one has seen God at any time'* (John 1:18), but there was something visible representing God.

It was mercy when God spoke to her (16:8). The 'angel of Yahweh' speaks so kindly that Hagar is led to trust him with her story. She makes no attempt to disguise who she is and what has happened to her.

It was mercy when God told her what to do (16:9). Hagar is told that she should return and submit to Sarai no matter what Sarai might do.

It was mercy when God gave her promises concerning her child (16:10–12). She had expected that her son, the seed of Abraham, would become a great nation and that her descendants would be as many as the sand on the seashore. However her son is not actually the one God had in mind. The true 'seed of Abram' will be Sarai's son. Yet the promise to Hagar is close to what she had hoped would come to her as Abram's wife. It echoes the promises of a numerous seed that God had given to Abram. She will have a son (16:11). He will be a highly individualistic person living where he likes and doing what he likes, and so clashing with everyone (16:12).

It was mercy when Hagar came into a new appreciation of God. Just as Abram had come to appreciate God as 'El Elyon' (14:22), so now Hagar comes to appreciate God as 'El Roi' ('God of Seeing') because, as she said, *'Truly here in this place I have seen him who looks after me'* (16:13). The precise place came to be known as Beer-Lahai-Roi (16:14). She had a son who was called Ishmael (16:15). He was born eleven years after Abraham had arrived in Canaan (16:15–16).

In the midst of jealousy, cruelty, irresponsibility, impatience, and abundant sinfulness, God's grace stepped into the life of the most despised slave girl, and showed her His kindliness. From that point on she would never forget what had happened to her. She now knew God as the one who had been caring for her all along. Sin was multiplying but grace was multiplying all the more.

# Chapter 18

## Establishing God's Covenant
### (Genesis 17:1–8)

God was displeased with Abram's foolish unbelief concerning the promise and his turning to Hagar instead, and God's displeasure leads to Him being silent. Fourteen years went by before God gave Abram another major revelation of His plans (see 16:16; 17:1). Eventually, when Ishmael was at least thirteen years old, God spoke again.

God is still offering Abram an oath. A 'covenant of generosity' is a relationship in which God offers to give a promise on oath. The promise will then be so firmly established that it is certain of fulfilment and cannot be reversed.

Yet there is a long delay between the incident with Hagar and the next occasion when God gives a major revelation to Abram. God was rather displeased with Abram's folly and it was a long time before He spoke again to Abram about establishing His promises.

1. **God's covenants need to be 'established'.** The covenant-oath is on offer. God keeps on describing the promise. The covenant ceremony has taken place. But the covenant is not fully completed since no verbal oath has been given. At this point God speaks of 'establishing' the covenant. The word in 17:2 is the Hebrew word often translated 'give' but it has the sense of 'deliver', 'grant', 'set up'. In 17:7 there is a different word which means 'establish' or 'cause to stand'. To 'establish' a covenant is to turn the offer into a certainty. At present promises have been given but they have not yet been 'obtained' (see Hebrews 11:33). They are genuinely intended. God does not lie and in that sense the promise is sure. But they still could be lost. Promises are inherited by faith and

patience, and they are lost by unbelief and impatience. The fact that God is speaking of 'establishing' a covenant is a proof that in Genesis 12–22 there is one covenant spread over the entire story of Abraham's life. It is on offer, but it has not yet been 'established'. There are two things in this matter in which it is impossible for God to lie (Hebrews 6:18), the promise and the oath. God was not lying when He gave the promise; it was sincerely intended. But if the offered-promise becomes a sworn-promise it is established! When God first gives the promise it is offered; when God gives the oath it is sealed and cannot be lost.

As God moves forward with Abram seeking to carry forward His purpose, there comes an unprecedented word of assurance, and an unprecedented call to godliness.

2. **God gives an unprecedented word of assurance when He reminds Abram He is 'El Shaddai'** (17:1). 'El Shaddai' is the main name for God used by Abraham, Isaac, and Jacob (see Exodus 6:3). When we study the way it is used it is clear that the name has the meaning of 'The God who is powerful to act when we are in a desperate situation', 'the God who is Almighty on behalf of the helpless'.

In Genesis 17:1, Abram has been promised a son, but the son has not been born. Now Abram is old. The name is used in a situation of desperate need. God promises to be 'El Shaddai'. Other occasions when the name is used are similar. In Genesis 28:3, Jacob was in bad trouble and was running away from home. 'El Shaddai' is the One who can bless. Again in Genesis 35:11 we find a patriarch in trouble. He again is in a crisis situation; he is about to meet his brother who had threatened to kill him. In Genesis 43:14 Jacob is having to release Benjamin. He has already lost Joseph (or so he thinks). Now it seems he will lose Benjamin. So he says 'May El Shaddai show you mercy'. In Genesis 48:3 Jacob is on his death bed and refers to the time when he was in such a terrible situation and 'El Shaddai' appeared to him. In Genesis 49:25 Jacob is giving his farewell blessing. He talks of Joseph (49:23) and refers to the time when he had been attacked by the family and by Potiphar's wife – but 'El Shaddai ... blesses you'.

There is a consistent pattern in the use of 'El Shaddai'. It means 'The God who is powerful to act when His people are in a desperate situation'.

3. **God gives an unprecedented call to godliness**. The covenant gets established as the believer reaches to a high level of godliness. Abram is asked to 'walk before' God, and to be 'perfect' (17:1b). To 'walk before' God means to act visibly and publicly as God's servant in loyalty, openness and integrity.

To be 'perfect' means to have every area of one's life beyond easy criticism. It is not absolute sinlessness. It is blamelessness, sincerity, straightforwardness.

God has not asked anything like this from Abram before. **God's grace and mercy was experienced by Abram long before God began making such high demands**. But now the high demands have come! If Abram wants the oath of God's blessing, he must walk before God and have every area of his life to be straightforward and honest.

4. **Abram is further motivated by fuller revelations of what God has in mind for him**. Progression in faith brings progress in God's revelations. After the incident of Hagar's pregnancy, it might be thought that Abram was not making much progress in faith. But God does not view the matter that way. Despite weaknesses and digressions Abram still is following after the promises of God. Even his mistakes are mistakes about getting the promises of God fulfilled.

In Genesis 17:2–9 the promise concerning numbers is repeated (17:2; see 13:16; 15:5). While Abram is in a passive position before God (17:3), further enlargement is given. Abram will be the father of many nations (17:4–6). God has a son for Sarai in mind, not merely the descendants of Ishmael (see 17:16). And the promise takes in the worldwide blessing that will finally come through Abram's seed (see 12:3; Romans 4:16–17). Abram will become a new person, being given a supernatural enabling. His name will be changed as a sign of the newness of his ability (17:5). The people of Abraham will extend into the far distant future. The covenant is to be 'an everlasting covenant' (17:7–8). This suggests that there are aspects to the promise that are more than local and temporary. We are dealing here with the eternal purpose of God.

The **realisation** of God's promises will involve Abram's high level of obedience. The vast description of the promise here is intended to motivate him. God motivates us to go after our inheritance, by assuring us of His mighty power and willingness to assist the weak, and by putting before us the greatness of the vision. Then we are to walk before Him and be blameless. A persistent walk of faith will lead us to inherit all that God has in mind for us. It was true for Abraham; it will be true for Abraham's children, those who belong to Jesus Christ.

# Chapter 19

## Circumcision

### (Genesis 17:9-14)

Abram is at the point in his life when God is making higher and higher demands on him. He is being lifted up into higher levels of spirituality and godliness. He must 'walk before God and be perfect'.

Another aspect of his obedience is now put to him. Covenants generally have a covenant sign, and God wants there to be a 'covenant sign' in His covenant with Abram. What is happening is that this covenant is being gradually carried forward. The relationship exists, the promises have been made. Now the covenant sign is introduced. God is bringing the covenant to pass. He is moving towards taking an oath.

All Christians are 'children of Abraham'. We follow in the footsteps of our father Abram. We too are in covenant with God. For us too there are covenant-signs. God is wanting to say to us also 'Now I know that you fear me' and pour out abundant blessings upon us in which we 'enter into rest' and inherit God's promises.

There was only one covenant with Abram. The story of its being given and inherited is spread over chapters 12–22 in the book of Genesis. Often covenants have one or more special covenant-signs. It might be a rainbow; it might be the sabbath. In the covenant with Abram, it is circumcision, a small surgical operation on the organ of reproduction in which some covering skin is cut away.

This is laid on Abram as an obligation, as one of the things that he must do to inherit the promises. God says to Abram

'Now you for your part shall keep my covenant, you and your seed after you throughout their generations'. To 'keep the covenant' partly means to obey the single rule of Genesis 17:2. He must walk before God and keep every area of his life pleasing to God. It also means that he is to keep the obligation that is just about to be laid on him. He must be circumcised and get the male members of his household circumcised and see that it becomes a permanent regulation for his descendants.

This is perhaps the point at which we should notice that Abram is not living under the law of Moses. Paul makes much of this in Galatians. He points out that Abraham lived four centuries before the law of Moses existed and so he could not possibly have been saved or sanctified or have received any blessing by keeping the Mosaic law. Christians are in the same position. We go back to Abraham, not to Moses. We are Abraham's children and we are justified, given life, given assurance of salvation and are led into the ways of holiness – all without the Mosaic law. The truth is Abraham had **one** law to keep: walk before Me and be perfect. He was meant to know by the Holy Spirit how to walk with God. Mosaic legislation was not needed for his personal relationship with God; it would only be needed when the nation of Israel came along which would include ungodly people. *'The law is not made for the righteous person, but for those who are lawless . . .'* (1 Timothy 1:9).

The whole of God's requirement is summed up in one 'rule': walk before Me and be perfect! First God told Abram about promises. God expected him to believe them. Now God is speaking to him about the kind of life he must live. The order is important. Grace comes first; God's demand comes second. 'Walk before Me . . . be perfect'. This is the only 'rule of life' that Abram ever gets. God's command today is not the Mosaic legislation. We are children of Abraham. God's demand comes to us in short-and-sharp summaries like the one Abram received. *'Be perfect'* (Matthew 5:48) – said Jesus, referring to the love-command. *'Abide in Me'*, He said (John 15:4). *'If there is any other commandment, it is summed up in this saying "You shall love your neighbour . . ."'* (Romans

13:9). We fulfil the law by walking in the Spirit and focusing on one demand. Abraham was living this way a long time ago. He was walking in the Spirit before the law existed. The moral aspects of the Mosaic law get fulfilled as we walk in the Spirit.

A further demand was that Abram and his people get circumcised. It is important to notice that circumcision gets added to the covenant at **this** point of the story. Circumcision symbolises the things that are happening at this stage of events.

1. **Circumcision is a sign of the covenant promises**. God calls it *'the sign of the covenant'* (17:11) between Him and Abram. God's covenant-signs are signs of what God will do before they are signs of what men and women must do. The rainbow was the sign of God's promise never to send another flood. Circumcision is a sign of God's promise that newness of life will come to Abram, and he will be empowered to cooperate with all that God is promising will happen. Circumcision is the sign of God's moving in grace towards men and women through the 'seed of Abraham'; only then – after God's grace – can it be a sign of human responsiveness.

2. **Circumcision was required as part of Abraham's responsiveness**. *'You shall keep the covenant'*, said God (17:9). Earlier, when God was giving promises, Abram was asleep (15:12) or he was prostrate and silent before God (17:3), but here is something which he must do. The covenant-promises will be superintended by God. God will bring them to pass. But before they come to pass, God requires certain things from Abram and this is one of them.

Circumcision is first and foremost the sign of God's moving in grace towards men and women, but Abram did have to get himself circumcised. Adam had a surgical operation performed on him while he was asleep (Genesis 2:21) but Abram was not asleep when the surgical operation of circumcision would be performed. He had to get himself circumcised.

The Christian is under the covenant-sign of water baptism. They are not identical or totally parallel, but they are both covenant signs and they both point to the seed of Abraham who is Jesus. One reason why every Christian should take to himself the covenant-sign of water-baptism is that it is simply a matter of obedience. God wanted Abram's responsiveness and obedience, and circumcision was one of His demands.

# Chapter 20

## The Seal of Abraham's Salvation

(Genesis 17:9–14)

Circumcision symbolised the things that were happening when Abram was ninety-nine years old, and when God was carrying forward His plans to give Abram an oath of blessing.

Circumcision is (1) first and foremost the sign of God's moving in grace and God's promises; also (2) it was a test of obedience.

3. **Circumcision was a sign of the human problem**. The fact that the sign was connected with the human organ of procreation is significant. It points to birth and what is inherited by birth. It points to inherited sinfulness. In popular thinking circumcision has connections with hygiene. Its use as a spiritual symbol suggested there was an inherited uncleanness in the human race that was spiritual rather than physical. It suggested that the 'heart' needed to be circumcised, and that an uncircumcised inward nature was the very essence of the human predicament.

4. **Circumcision, then, speaks of God's willingness to give a new heart to enable obedience**. Only those with a circumcised heart can obey God. Circumcision signifies consecration. This is why we have phrases like that in Jeremiah 4:4 *'Circumcise yourself to the LORD ... '*. When Abraham remembered the day when God imposed circumcision on him, he remembered it was the day when God said *'Walk before Me ... Be perfect'*. A person with a new heart, a new nature, has been purged of dominating and domineering uncleanness. He is in a position to obey God. Circumcision was a sign of new birth.

5. But it is not merely 'birth'; **circumcision also speaks of continuing and progressive renewal**. God gave Abram a new name many years after he had come to faith. *'Your name shall be Abraham'*, said God (17:5). The new name meant that at this point God was giving Abram an ability he had never had before. He was being given new power to conceive Isaac the miracle child. God was bestowing on him the ability to be 'Abraham' – the father of a multitude. Circumcision spoke of newness of nature, but that new nature could receive deeper and fuller renewals and enablings as time went on.

6. Circumcision spoke of **God's willingness to come to the aid of those with a new name and new nature**. 'I am El Shaddai' was a promise accompanying the call to newness of life. God is willing to work in assisting those who are aspiring for high levels of spirituality and faith. When Abraham remembered his circumcision he would remember too the occasion when God promised His assistance in newness of living. The name 'El Shaddai' lets Abraham know that he not only has a new ability; he has the God who is Almighty on behalf of the needy, the God who is powerful to act when extra help is needed.

7. Circumcision was thus **a call to obedience**. Abraham would never be able to forget that God came to him with renewed promises despite the failure of his faith in connection with Hagar. Yet the time with renewed promises was also a time of a new and more explicit call to obedience. Abraham must *'keep the covenant'* (17:9, 10). He must be circumcised and remember everything that God laid upon him at this time. Without obedience his circumcision meant nothing. God has clothed him with righteousness, made him a new person, given him new power, but this is all with the intent that Abraham will be responsive to God more than ever.

8. **Circumcision was a sign that salvation was coming through Israel**. Circumcision amongst other things marked out a people and eventually a nation. Abraham's descendants as an earthly people were characterised by circumcision. This pin-pointed the significance of the nation in the history of salvation. Salvation is of the Jews. Abraham was told to circumcise everyone who had a physical or social connection

with the family of Abraham. He has to circumcise every male (17:10), including slaves and foreigners (17:12–13). Salvation will come in the line of Abraham's descendants. Circumcision marks out Abraham's community. It will be among them that the one will come through whom there will be worldwide blessing. Unlike water-baptism, circumcision was (amongst other things) the sign of membership in an earthly people, the line of Abraham, and later the nation of Israel.

9. **Circumcision was a sign that Abraham's way of salvation was the only way of salvation**. It said to anyone who wanted to know, 'What has taken place in Abraham's line is the only way to salvation and renewal and godliness'. It was this that made Abraham the father of all believers. It marked out Abraham as the model of salvation, the model believer. God was in covenant first with Abraham. Others were only in covenant (at one level) if they descended from Abraham or (at another level) if they shared his faith. Circumcision told them all: 'follow Abraham's way'. His way of salvation – by faith and more faith and more faith – was the way of salvation and the way of renewal so as to inherit the promises.

10. **Circumcision was a seal to Abraham personally**. For Abraham himself it sealed his salvation. It said to Abraham, 'This is a confirmation that what has been happening to you so far is right. This is the way of salvation. Persist in faith and the inheritance will come.' It is no accident that the New Testament says circumcision 'seals' the righteousness Abraham had by faith (Romans 4:11). In the life of the Christian the 'sealing' is the outpouring of the Holy Spirit (Ephesians 1:13, 14). When circumcision was given, that was for Abraham an infallible assurance of his salvation. The equivalent for later believers was not circumcision (for circumcision 'sealed' Abraham's salvation not that of anyone else). It was not water-baptism, which certainly does not 'seal' salvation. The 'seal' is the Spirit Himself. Circumcision is in **this** respect the equivalent in the life of Abraham of the baptism with the Holy Spirit.

When Abraham was given circumcision it sealed his justification, symbolised his new birth, and called him to heights of obedience. The event that does the same thing in the Christian's life is the 'sealing' of the Holy Spirit. The Christian no longer needs circumcision. He has a circumcised heart from Jesus and he has the sealing of the Holy Spirit.

# Chapter 21

# Riches of Mercy

(Genesis 17:15–27)

The person for whom one sympathizes the most in the Book of Genesis is Sarai. God had been dealing mainly with Abraham. Initially Abraham and Sarai must have assumed that the child would come through them both, but there was no special word for Sarai.

1. **God shows mercy to Sarai**. Most of us have at some time been in a situation where everybody else seems to be being blessed by God but not us! Maybe God is working in a very distinctive way and there are certain manifestations of His presence but we seem to have been passed by. This is what was happening to Sarai. Everything seemed to be happening to Abraham and nothing was happening to her.

God is totally sovereign in the way He gives His promises and in the way He deals with people in great variety. For over twenty years God gave promises to Abraham but none to Sarai!

After a few years Abraham started talking about adopting a son! He was beginning to believe that Sarai never would have any child and was thinking about adopting Eliezar, his manservant, as his son (15:2). Some years later Sarai had lost all hope of ever having the child that was promised and it was her idea that Abraham should get a child through Hagar (16:2).

Abraham was ninety-nine years old (17:1), and Sarai was eighty-nine (17:17). God appeared to Abraham and called him to high levels of obedience (17:1–2). Abraham responded with gratitude and awe (17:3) and then God enlarged the promise. God's promises were renewed. The seed of Abraham would become a multitude of nations (17:4). Abraham would be given the ability to be the father of the seed (17:5). A new fruitfulness would come even into his body (17:6). Kings would be among Abraham's descendants and the promised blessings would go on for ever (17:6–7). All the land of Canaan would be given to his descendants (17:8). Then God called Abraham to make sure that the sign of the covenant, circumcision, was carried out for every man in Abraham's community (17:9–14).

Now there comes a further message for Abraham and now at long, long last it has a word of promise for Sarai (17:15–16)! God not only has a new name for Abraham. He has a new name for Sarai as well; from now on she will be not Sarai but Sarah. The names are two different forms of a word meaning 'Princess'. It is as though God were saying 'Now she really will be a Princess'!

God is sovereign in the way He works and He never promises to deal with everyone alike. Yet when God 'neglects' a person for a while, His blessing when it comes is all the greater. Actually, Sarah received a far greater miracle in her life than Abraham. It is not so miraculous for a hundred-year-old man to conceive a son, but who ever heard of an ninety-year-old woman having a baby! God kept Sarah waiting but when at last He did something unusual for her it was greater than anything Abraham or Hagar or anyone else had ever heard about. God worked sovereignly and mercifully in Sarah's life as well as in Abraham's. He totally forgave her foolishness and impatience in offering her maid to Abraham, and despite all her mistakes the promise came to her as well as to Abraham.

2. **God shows mercy to Abraham**. Despite his serious unbelief in going to Hagar, God had mercy on him. The lengthy silence that Abraham had to endure was a sign of God's displeasure, but all is forgiven, and God picks up with Abraham again.

Abraham responds with worship and with laughter (17:17). He falls on his face in admiration and worship at the amazing ways of God. He is laughing with joy and astonishment. He is lifted up with glorious and triumphant happiness. After a lifetime of waiting at last the promise is about to be fulfilled.

Yet Abraham is not completely ready for such a sudden answer to his hopes. He had got used to things being as they were, for he had still been entertaining the idea that Ishmael would be the fulfilment of God's promises. So when a son for Sarah is promised, Abraham says *'O that Ishmael might live before you!'* (17:18). Abraham has got so used to thinking of Ishmael as 'the seed', that he is not quite ready for the promise to come through Sarah. He has got into the habit of being content with something less than what God intended. He is not rejecting God's promise of a son for Sarah yet in his confusion he wants Ishmael to be 'the seed' as well.

God gives two answers. The first is 'I mean what I say.[1] Your wife Sarah will bear you a son, and you will call him Isaac (*"He laughs"*). I will establish my covenant with him...' (17:19). Despite all the wanderings and ups-and-downs in Abraham's life God plans to bless him. Isaac will soon be born. God is still offering to 'establish' the covenant through him (17:19). The second answer concerns Ishmael. Abraham has become fond of Ishmael and all his hopes have been wrapped up in him. He has been Abraham's only son for more than thirteen years. Is Ishmael to be rejected? It is a question to which we shall return (see Genesis 25:12–18, and the last chapter of this book) but God gives an answer straightaway. Ishmael will be blessed by God but will not be in the line leading to Jesus, the seed of Abraham (17:20). The covenant will be established through Isaac (17:21).

God shows such mercy to Abraham and partially gives Abraham his wishes. He has a future for Ishmael. Although Abraham's folly in turning to Hagar is not going to make God change His mind about Isaac, yet God plans to *'work all things together for good'*. Genesis 17:18 will be answered more than in our wildest dreams. The people of Ishmael still exist. The modern Arab nations are their descendants. Not only does the nation of Israel still exist, the people of Ishmael still exist as well! If God has ultimate plans to save 'all Israel' (Romans 11:25–26), surely God has plans that 'Ishmael might live' as well! If Israel will be blessed *'beloved for the sake of their ancestors'* (Romans 11:28), surely the Arab peoples will be blessed as well, beloved for the sake of Abraham who prayed for them. The amazing mercy of God to Abraham will be seen to have a greater fulfilment than ever. When the 'fullness of the Gentiles' comes in (Romans 11:12), the people of Ishmael will be there also.

The revelation comes to an end (17:22) and Abraham carries out the instruction concerning circumcision for the household (17:23) and for Ishmael (17:24–25). The chapter closes with a note concerning his thorough obedience in the matter (17:26–27). It is a chapter in which God's sovereignty and grace stand out. He is capable of working all things together for good. He can bless us after long delay and shattered hopes. He can overrule our follies and our stupidities. *'God has imprisoned all in disobedience so that He may be merciful to all'* (Romans 11:32).

## Footnote

[1] The Hebrew word used here is translated 'Yes' by the New International Version (NIV), and 'No' by the New Revised Standard Version (NRSV)! The sense is 'I mean what I say!'

# Chapter 22

## Calling the Promise Into Being
### (Genesis 18:1–15)

Some strangers arrive at Abraham's rural home at a time when it is very hot (18:1). He greets them with extreme respect, running to meet them and showing great courtesy (18:2). He pleads with them to stay awhile (18:3) and sends for a bowl of water to wash their feet, urging them to rest under a tree (18:4). They accept his offer, and while they are resting Abraham arranges for food to be cooked for them. Behind the scenes the women get on with the cooking for the new arrivals (18:5–6). One of the young animals from the herd is killed to obtain meat (18:7) and a few hours later the guests are served. Abraham does not eat with them. He stands by them, more like a servant than a sharer in the meal (18:8).

It is a classic description of hospitality. Abraham did not at first realise who they were. He was serving angels *'without knowing it'* (Hebrews 13:2). With a few changes (the water might be for the hands rather than the feet, and the animal might be a goat rather than a calf) it is typical of rural Africa and of many parts of the third world today, but it is not at all like Europe or America! What is interesting is that the writer of Hebrews 13:2 had this passage in mind when he wrote *'Do not neglect to show hospitality to strangers, for by so doing some have entertained angels without knowing it'*. **One of Abraham's greatest blessings came while he was being hospitable in the midst of ordinary life**. He entertained angels without knowing it because he took it for granted that hospitality was important.

While the strangers were relaxing there came a casual question. *'Where is Sarah?'* (18:9). It was startling. They knew her new name! Then their identity became more obvious because one of them began to speak as if he were God! *'I will surely return to you according to the time of life and behold there will be a son for Sarah your wife'* (18:10). The phrase *'according to the time of life'* does not mean 'in due season' or 'about this time next year', but refers to the period of gestation. Sarah is to become pregnant in the next few days and 'according to time it takes for life to come to full birth' the child will be born. This understanding of the text is confirmed by 2 Kings 4:16–17 where a woman is told that in about a years' time she will embrace a son 'according to the time of life'. It will take nine months and more before the child will be in her arms. The phrase 'according to the time of life' again refers to a period of gestation and the next verse puts it clearly. The woman became pregnant, and bore a son at the same season of the year a few months after the birth *'according to the time it takes for life to come to full birth'* (2 Kings 4:17).

What this means is that the miracle of conception will take place within a few days. The child will be a miracle-child; however it will **not** be a virgin birth like the birth of Jesus! The child will be conceived in the normal way except that God will be making the conception possible. In one sense Isaac will be born of the flesh; sexual union will be involved. But in another sense Isaac will be produced by the Holy Spirit because God will be working a miracle. Yet the miracle-child will take nine months to be born like any other child. This is why Paul can use Isaac as a case of a child *'born according to the Spirit'* (Galatians 4:29). It also relates to Paul's teaching concerning predestination. The teaching is that God **produces** His elect. God is choosing to use Isaac to be the one who carries forward His covenant. Isaac is being *'born through the promise'* (Galatians 4:23). **The promise produces its own children!** *'It is through Isaac that your seed shall be called into being'* (Romans 9:7).[1]

**Sarah is blessed by God despite the weakness of her faith**. She was listening behind the tent door (10:10b). The couple are advanced in age (18:11) and Sarah giggles in sceptical wonderment (18:12) but is rebuked by the all-knowing angel

(18:13). Yet Sarah is blessed by God despite the weakness of her faith. Abraham's laughter seems to have been the laughter of joy. Sarah's laughter was sceptical. She had many, many times before been hoping that God's promise would come about. Was it really about to happen now? She is a bit cynical. Yet she is rebuked by God ('*Is anything too hard...?*') and she becomes afraid of having disbelieved an angel. In her fear she denies that she even said what she did (18:14–15). But her heart is right and we must sympathize with her. She is in her nineties and has had a life with many sufferings in it.

In the event Sarah came to trust the promise. Her faith rose above her doubts, and the Bible is emphatic that by faith she bore the child (see 21:1–2). She believed God's word. Blessing came to Sarah is the course of her being hospitable and living a life of practical godliness. It came despite great delay. It came despite weakness of faith.

God was not blessing **great** faith in Sarah, but he was blessing **real** faith. It comes to us as an encouragement to go on believing God. She experienced severe sufferings, long delay, unstable faith, and the weakness of old age – but God brought her through everything and she achieved God's purpose for her life.

## Footnote

[1] See D.M. Lloyd-Jones' magnificent book, *Romans: God's Sovereign Purpose* (Banner of Truth, 1991), pp. 108–115, and M.A. Eaton, *Predestination and Israel* (Paternoster, 1999), ch. 7.

# Chapter 23

## Abraham's Intercession
### (Genesis 18:16–33)

One great aspect of the life of faith is prayer, and Abraham is a model in this respect as he is in almost every aspect of the Christian life.

Genesis 18:16–33 is the first lengthy prayer of the Bible, but it is not the first time prayer is mentioned. God spoke with man in the garden of Eden. Adam after the fall (Genesis 3:12) and even Cain (4:9) both talked to God. Public worship began at an early stage of the human race (Genesis 4:26) and Enoch kept up a continual fellowship with God that is called 'walking with God' (Genesis 5:21–24). God spoke to Abraham, and Abraham called on the name of Yahweh (Genesis 12:1–3, 7; 13:4, 18) and took specific matters to God in prayer (15:2, 3). He prayed a one-line prayer in Genesis 17:18 but now we see Abraham engaged in more sustained and lengthy praying.

The angels are on their way to Sodom. Three of them have visited Abraham and Sarah (18:1); now two of them go on to Sodom (19:1) but the 'angel of Yahweh' stays behind. The 'angel of Yahweh' is God Himself manifesting Himself as an angel. This angel can be called 'God' because this manifestation is a special representation of God. Abraham is seeing the angels on their way (18:16), and Yahweh is considering sharing His secret with Abraham, (18:17). God has chosen him and has plans to bring him to a high level of godliness, in order to fulfil the promises that have been given through him (18:18–19). God plans to investigate Sodom (18:20–21) and do whatever needs to be done (18:20–21).

1. **Intercession is part of leadership**. If Abraham is to be a

great and significant figure in the story of salvation, then he must be an intercessor. All great leaders are great pray-ers. 'Intercessors' are never mentioned in the Bible as a special set of church officers. All Christians are to be intercessors and Christian leaders especially should have a warm heart towards the needs of others and should show their tenderness by being intercessors. God gives Abraham the opportunity to take the burden of a doomed city upon his own heart. Leaders are to be 'the people's representative before God' (Exodus 18:19, speaking of Moses). They 'bring their case' before the Lord (see Numbers 27:5). The is the picture of great leaders throughout the Bible (see Exodus 32:30–32; Deuteronomy 9:18–19; 1 Kings 13:6; 2 Kings 19:4; Jeremiah 7:16; 11:14; 14:11; John 17; Ephesians 1:15–19, and elsewhere).

2. **Intercessory prayer is one of the most unselfish things you can ever do**. Many aspects of serving God can be a little selfish. We enjoy ourselves and maybe we get a bit of appreciation. Preaching especially is rewarding and satisfying to those who are called to preach. But nothing is as unselfish as intercessory prayer! Abraham is not living in Sodom. The judgement of God that is about to fall will not in any way touch him. It is sheer unselfish generosity and goodness when he intercedes for the city.

3. **Intercessory prayer is one of the most humble things you can ever do, if you do not mention it**. Many aspects of God's service are public, but intercession should be a fairly secret matter. An intercessor who publicizes that he or she is an intercessor is missing part of the blessing. You don't *'love to stand and pray in the synagogues and on the street corners'* (Matthew 6:5). The reward comes when you *'go into your inner room, and when you have shut the door'* (Matthew 6:6). Abraham was alone when he interceded for Sodom. Maybe he kept a diary and told the story eventually (for we now have the report in Genesis!) but at the time it was secret praying.

4. **It is a very great privilege if God shares His prayer burden with you**. As Abraham is saying farewell to the three angelic guests, God is considering the possibility of sharing His burden with His friend Abraham. He is a very hospitable person and is escorting his guests as they leave (18:16). One of

the angels is especially representing God. God Himself is appearing as an angel. No one can actually see God but angels can represent God visually.

One aspect of the mystery of prayer is the way in which God always maintains the initiative. The angels go on their way but the angel of God stays behind. The narrative is compressed but we are clearly meant to understand that God puts the matter to Abraham. Then Abraham starts pleading for mercy for the city of Sodom on account of the righteous people who might be in it. God puts a matter to Abraham and waits to see what he will do. This is the way it is when we are *'praying in the Holy Spirit'*. God takes the initiative. He puts things before us by the Holy Spirit and waits to see what we shall do.

God may share secrets with us. He may give us a fore-knowledge of what is about to happen. When God does this it is not always that we might tell out to the world what He is about to do. When God gives us this high privilege the purpose is often that we might pray. Sometimes God can reveal something that **could** happen in order that we might pray that it will **not** happen (as in Amos 7:1–3).

God also stays in control of the praying. He stays there before Abraham as long as He wishes to, while Abraham is interceding (18:22–32), and then God *'finished speaking with Abraham'* and *'departed'*. Notice it does not say 'Abraham finished talking with God'; it says God finished speaking with Abraham. This is part of the mystery of prayer. Although **we** are doing the praying, it is still true that God is mysteriously in control of it. This is part of what it means to pray 'in the Spirit'. He puts before us the subject to be prayed about. And He is in control at the beginning, in the middle and He determines when the praying should end.

# Chapter 24

## Intercessory Prayer
### (Genesis 18:16–33)

There are different kinds of praying. There is worship or adoration, in which we express our loving admiration for God. There is confession, in which we admit of sinfulness and confess what we have done that has damaged fellowship with God. There is petition and supplication, in which we throw ourselves upon God for our needs. There is thanksgiving, when we tell God how grateful we are for things He has done for us. But there is another special kind of praying: intercession, praying for the needs of others.

There is a special blessing for us if we are intercessors. Intercessory prayer is not just something which a special elite number of believers have as their special hobby. It is for all Christians. It is part of being a 'child of Abraham'. When Abraham interceded for the barren women of Abimelech, he immediately received a blessing himself; the barrenness of his own wife came to an end (Genesis 20:17–21:2). It was his intercessory praying for others that led God to answer the prayer he had been praying for himself. *'God restored the fortunes of Job, when he prayed for his friends'*, says Job 42:10.

5. **True praying begins with 'drawing near'**. Abraham drew near to God, says Genesis 18:23. The first thing you do when you pray is 'draw near'. It means that by faith you set foot into the throne room of God. You 'come into His presence'. Of course God is present everywhere and all the time, yet there is such a thing as 'drawing near' to God. The best way to know what it is, is to do it! It is when you 'in spirit' are coming before God. You know that He is listening to you. You are confident that He will hear you and listen to the prayers and

praises, the requests and the arguments that you are about to put to Him.

6. **True praying is argumentative**. It is noticeable that Abraham presents reasons and arguments to God. *'Surely you would not be unjust!'* he says to God (23:25). God does not mind if we press Him and give Him plenty of reasons why we want our prayers answered.

7. **True praying is a mixture of boldness and humility**. Abraham boldly moves from point to point, asking God for more and more. He is daring in the way he prays.

And yet he is humble and feels that he is asking a lot *'I am dust and ashes'*, he says (18:27). *'Please let not the Lord be angry'* (18:30). *'Let not the Lord be angry; I will speak yet once more'* (18:32).

The Bible says that God is a *'consuming fire'* and yet it also tells us to come to Him boldly! How can one come with boldness to a consuming fire? Yet that is what we are asked to do.

8. **There is such a thing as 'progressive' praying**. Abraham gives us a good example here. He moves from point to point, asking for more and more. When he has got one part of his answer he proceeds to the next. Why should we pray in this way? It is a help to our faith. Very often we do not feel we can ask for something all in one go. We find it easier to pray for some lesser thing and when God has heard us, then we have the faith to pray for something greater. We rise higher and higher as we pray, and we find that we have faith for greater requests. The answer to one part of praying gives us faith to ask for something more and greater. It is 'progressive praying'.

9. **We must be ready for God to answer us as He wishes**. We might ask the question: did God answer this prayer? In the next chapter, despite all of Abraham's praying, Sodom was destroyed. So what was the value of Abraham's praying for the righteous in Sodom?

One answer is that there were not ten righteous people in Sodom! Abraham stopped praying – or the Lord stopped him from praying – for anything greater than the withholding of judgement if there were ten righteous people in the city.

But the righteous were rescued. Lot's rescue by the angels (Genesis 19:16) was surely the result of Abraham's praying. Lot was actually lingering and hoping that the city would not be destroyed. He was an inconsistent believer who rather liked the city of Sodom. God could easily have let him perish in the city with the wicked people he had chosen to live with. But God had mercy on him, as Genesis 19:16 says.

What it means is that we must be ready for God to answer us as He wishes. His answer may come in a different form from what we imagined.

In his willingness to be an intercessor Abraham is like Jesus, because the greatest intercessor of all time is Jesus. He is interceding for us even now. Every Christian can know that Jesus is at the right hand of the Father interceding for him. It is not that Jesus is begging but He is saying something to God for us and it is a request. It is right to call it 'interceding'.

Jesus prays for exactly the right things for us. He prays that we might be kept from being captured by Satan, that we might be kept in unity, that our faith might continue. The reason why the Christian survives at all is because he has a great Intercessor. Yet Jesus' interceding is also done through His church. By His Spirit He leads us to pray for each other, and so as well as His own intercession He does some interceding through us also.

Praying for others in this way is one of the greatest things we can ever do. It identifies with God and with Jesus. It is truly Christlike. In this respect, as in many others, we are to be 'children of Abraham'.

# Chapter 25

## Saved Through Fire

(Genesis 19:1–9)

The story of the destruction and annihilation of Sodom and Gomorrah and its surrounding areas is the second great example of the outpoured wrath of God in the Bible – the first being the story of the flood.

1. **Society can deteriorate until the judgement of God becomes inevitable and unstoppable**. God will often leave a society in its sins for a while, without destroying it. But eventually a society may become so bad that God resolves to act.

Widespread homosexual practices in a culture is a sign of the nearness of judgement upon that culture. God's judgement on Sodom was getting slowly nearer and nearer. Sodom and Gomorrah are about to be punished because of their sinful and wicked ways. God allows sin to go unjudged for a long time. It is a mistake that Christians sometimes make when they imagine that the righteous will be immediately blessed and that the wicked will be immediately punished. It often does not work that way. God's rewards are often delayed and God's judgements are often delayed. Sodom had been tolerated by God but now it is getting towards the end of its history. God is going to wipe it out of existence. Practising homosexuality is referred to elsewhere in the Bible in addition to Genesis 19 (see Leviticus 18:22; 20:13; Judges 19; Romans 1:26, 27; 1 Corinthians 6:9–11; 1 Timothy 1:9–10). It is portrayed always as a great evil. Romans chapter 1 lists different stages in the decay of a nation. When a country turns from natural sin to unnatural sin, and tolerates homosexual practices, God's judgement is not far away. Luke

95

17:28–30 lets us know that this is how it will be towards the end of the world.

2. **It is tragic when the children of God get caught up in the world's judgement**. Angels come to judge the city and to warn Lot and then to pour out God's judgement upon it (19:1a). Lot is sitting in the gateway of the city. He now is very much at home in Sodom and feels that he is a prominent citizen there. The 'gateway' was the place where important people did their business.

We are warned in Scripture that it is possible to get involved in the world's sins but when we do, we get involved in the world's judgement. Paul warns against *'immorality ... impurity ... greed ... filthiness ... '* and says *'Because of these things the wrath of God is coming upon the sons of disobedience'* (Ephesians 5:3–4, 6). *'Therefore'*, he says *'do not be partakers of them'* (Ephesians 5:7). If the Christian partakes of the world's sins he will partake of the world's judgement. He will be 'hurt' by the second death (Revelation 2:11).

Lot is not doing much good in Sodom. He does not have a powerful testimony in Sodom. Abraham did more for Sodom out of it than Lot did in it. Abraham had once helped Sodom when he rescued his nephew from the kings of the east (Genesis 14:1–24). He had prayed for Sodom (Genesis 18:16–33). God asked Abraham to intercede for Sodom, yet He did not ask Lot to intercede for it.

Lot greets the 'men' politely and invites them to his home (19:1b–2a). They want to spend the night outside (19:2b) but Lot knows this will be dangerous (19:3). At night time the male population of the city gather around the house (19:4).

Lot had steadily declined in spirituality. It all began when he decided he wanted to be rich. In Genesis 13:1–13 we read of a time of dispute between Abraham's and Lot's employees. Lot decided he wanted the richer and more luxurious part of the country, but he chose to live near Sodom (13:12), without regard for the spiritual danger involved.

A little later we find him living in Sodom (14:12). He had fully settled down in a wicked city, and was feeling quite at home there. Sometimes people want to move to a richer country. But often they are moving into spiritual danger when they are ambitious in that way. Most Christians who move home to another country in order to get rich lose their spirituality. They focus on getting rich but find it hard to enter the kingdom of God. Abraham had a tent. Lot had a house (19:3). Abraham was living for a heavenly city; Lot was living for an earthly city.

The streets of Sodom were not safe at night and Lot knew it. Soon it becomes clear that a man was not safe in his home either. The male population of the city arrived and soon were banging on Lot's door. They want to abuse the new arrivals in town (19:4–5).

They are persistent and shameless. Lot's pleas do no good (19:6–8). Lot has no influence with these people at all (19:9). He may have gone to Sodom with the idea that he would be a good witness to God in the city, but it had not worked out that way at all. A compromiser is never a good witness.

3. **Lot is rescued despite all of his compromising ways**. *'God knows how to rescue the godly'* says 2 Peter 2:9, having just said *'God rescued Lot, a righteous man'* (2:7). If Peter had not said it we might not have thought that Lot was righteous at all!

So Lot was saved – but he was *'saved by fire'* (1 Corinthians 3:15). He did not lose his salvation but he lost just about everything else. He lost his usefulness, his honour, his happiness. He lost his wife. His children were a disgrace to him. Being *'saved through fire'* is a terrible thing. Better to get out of 'Sodom' fast. If Lot had got out of the city earlier and started living for God, he could have been restored. The way of forgiveness and restoration stays open for a long time, but then one day the angels of judgement come, and we start reaping what we have sown. God rescued 'righteous Lot' but it would have been better if he had never been there in the first place.

# Chapter 26

## Sodom and Gomorrah
### (Genesis 19:10–38)

Lot is rescued from the violent men of Sodom. The angels pull him back into the house (19:10), and the men are struck by some kind of blindness (19:11). Perhaps like the story in 2 Kings 6:18–20 it is not so much literal blindness as a confusion of mind that makes it impossible for the person to know where he is. It soon becomes clear that Lot has no influence on his family (19:12–14). When he tries to warn his sons they think he is joking. How can a man who has chosen to come to Sodom give anyone a warning about living there?

Lot is reluctant to believe that his beloved Sodom is going to be punished. He hangs around hoping that it might not be true after all and that he might be allowed to stay there after all. Perhaps God will change His mind! But Sodom is not Jonah's Nineveh! Jonah's Nineveh could repent; Sodom was beyond repentance. The angels have to drag Lot away (19:15–16). Then they give a stern warning. *'Get as far away from Sodom as you can!'*, they say (19:17). But Lot wants a little bit of the Sodom-life! There is a little town not far away. Please – he asks – can this little bit of the Sodom-area be saved just for me? *'Is it not a little one?'* (19:18–20). Lot is deeply immersed in the life of a wicked city. He gets what he wants but it is not worth having (19:21–23).

Then God's judgement comes. It totally annihilates the city and the surrounding area (19:24–25). Lot's wife looked back. She shares in the judgement of the city (19:26). The next day when the annihilation is all over there is nothing left but the ascending smoke. The *'smoke of their torment'* is going up even though the act of destruction is finished (19:27–28). The cities have been *'destroyed'* (19:29). Abraham is safe. Lot has been *'saved through fire'*. Lot's wife has not exactly shared in the fate of the doomed city but she has lost her life.

The last nine verses tell us of the end of Lot's story. He lives in fear. He never did live in his chosen Zoar although it was his 'intercession' for it that caused it to be spared (19:30). He had lost everything, his wife, his home, his possessions, and was soon to lose his morality, his dignity and his reputation. Let it never be said that being *'saved through fire'* is an easy option. The way of a transgressor is hard, and the way of a believing transgressor is worse. 'Righteous' Lot was certainly a believer and we shall meet him in heaven, but he ended his life in a terrible way. His daughters get him drunk (19:31) and he commits drunken incest with his daughters (19:32–36). The Moabites and Ammonites were his offspring (19:37–38).

'Sodom and Gomorrah' is a sample of what God's judgement is like. *'As it was in the days of Lot … it will be like that on the day that the Son of Man is revealed'* (Luke 17:28–30).

1. **It is a picture of eternal punishment**. God's fire and sulphur which destroyed Sodom is what will be used on the day of judgement. *'Sodom and Gomorrah'*, says Jude, *' … serve as a sample by undergoing a punishment of eternal fire'* (Jude 7). Deuteronomy speaks of *'soil burned out by sulphur and salt, with nothing planted, nothing sprouting, and unable to support any vegetation, like the destruction of Sodom and Gomorrah'* (Deuteronomy 29:23). It was a foretaste of hell.

2. **It is a picture of being 'saved through fire'**. Lot was brought through the fire and it was not allowed to destroy him in the way that it destroyed the others. Yet Lot will never have the honour that will come to those who have lived a godly life. I doubt whether Jesus will say 'Well done, good and faithful servant' to Lot.

3. It includes **an example of a believer losing her life because of extreme rebelliousness**. I suppose Lot's wife was a believer in the promises concerning Abraham's seed. Lot's wife was part of the family of Abraham that had in faith left Haran. She was willing, evidently, to move from Haran and travel with her husband to Canaan. But when Sodom was under threat she revealed that she had drifted a long way away from

God. She wanted to be in Sodom, and was looking back grieving over what she had lost. She did not share the fate of Sodom; God rescued her. That makes it clear that she was one of God's people. Yet she was guilty of extreme rebelliousness in disobeying a clear instruction not to look back to Sodom. God took her life, not to send her to hell, but to mark out His extreme displeasure when His people look back to worldly ways. *'My soul takes no pleasure in anyone who shrinks back'* (Hebrews 10:38). Lot's wife lost her life. Even that does not prove she went to hell. She can be included with Ananias and Sapphira and the Christian brothers and sisters of 1 Corinthians 11:30 who were taken prematurely to heaven because God wished to show how He felt about the sin of hypocrisy (Ananias and Sapphira) or ill-treatment of the poorer Christian (1 Corinthians 11:21–22, 29–30), or (as in Genesis 19) an extreme fondness for the world and its ways.

Strangely, there is something encouraging about the story of Lot. It is the greatest example of an inconsistent believer getting to heaven anywhere in the Bible. Peter is quite clear that 'righteous' Lot was rescued (2 Peter 2:7–9). God did not save him from judgement and then send him to hell! Lot is in heaven now! There were not ten righteous men in the city, but Lot was a believer and that was enough for God to save him.

# Chapter 27

## Unexpected Weakness
### (Genesis 20:1–18)

After the destruction of Sodom and Gomorrah, Abraham travelled towards the Negev, in the south of Israel. He journeys to the area between Kadesh (in the south of Canaan) and Shur (in the Sinai peninsula), and then he turns to the northwest and stays for a while in Gerar.

While in Gerar he does the same thing as he had done in Egypt many years before.

It is like the story of Abraham and Pharaoh (see 12:10–20) all over again, though there are many differences (the places, the kings, their characters, the circumstances, the way in which the kings find out the truth, the reactions of Abraham, and the final attitude of the kings, are all different).

1. **Abraham was confronted again by weakness in his character**. After the tremendous call to godliness in Genesis 17:1–2, and the great praying of Genesis 18:16–33, we expect the life of Abraham to go rapidly forward and we expect that we shall soon be told the story of the birth of the miracle-child. But to our surprise we find Abraham falling back into the same old weakness that we have read about at the beginning of his story (see 12:10–20). He seems to have made little progress since the days of his first arrival in Canaan! Worse still, having just been told clearly that it will be Sarah that will give birth to the miracle-child, he now risks the birth of the child by letting Sarah be taken into the harem of another pagan king.

The result is the same as before! Abimelech, like Pharaoh, takes Sarah into his harem (20:2). She is older than before and is no longer called beautiful (contrast 12:11), but even in her nineties she is good looking! The ages of Abraham and Sarah are perplexing. Either their lives are spread out to about twice their natural length, in which case Sarah is the equivalent of a 45-year old mature woman. Or some kind of number system based on six rather than ten, is being used, in which case Sarah is the equivalent of a 54-year old woman. Whichever way it is, she is good looking!

God warns Abimelech in a dream (20:3), and Abimelech is eager to clear himself (20:4–5). Although as a matter of sheer fact he has sinned, it was totally unintentional (which lets us know that sin can be committed when there is no knowledge of it and no sinful intention. Sin is an objective matter; it is not just a question of intention).

God had protected Abimelech and had protected Sarah (20:6–7). Abimelech explains what has happened to the royal household (20:8), rebukes Abraham for his deceit and demands an explanation (20:9–10). Abraham makes feeble excuses (20:11–13). Abimelech gives many gifts to Abraham, gives Sarah back and invites Abraham to live where he wants in his territory (20:14–15). He apologises to Sarah (20:16). Finally Abraham prays for the wives of Abimelech who had become barren during this period. They are healed and all is well (20:17–18).

It is a rebuke to Abraham's persistent proneness to deceit. We have all made mistakes, and we have all made the same mistake more than once! We are slow to learn, and have weak points which lead us astray again and again. Our weak points need firm handling. They need to be eradicated firmly and permanently. Abraham is showing an area where he is not 'walking before Yahweh'. One would think that the disgrace that fell on Abraham in Egypt (12:10–20) would be enough for him to know that God was not blessing his trick about pretending Sarah was his sister. But he has not yet faced his proneness to needless deceit, and his inconsiderateness towards Sarah.

2. **Abraham was again guilty of needless suspicion**. Abraham took it for granted, without any real foundation for his suspicions, that Abimelech would kill Abraham. Often the ungodly are not as ungodly as one might think, and the godly

are not as godly as one might think! Actually Abimelech is more honest, generous and courteous in these events than one would have expected. In Sodom there was great wickedness but in Gerar the king, although having a harem, lived in the fear of God (20:11). Lot imagined there was some good in Sodom and was badly mistaken. Abraham imagined that the rulers of Gerar would be murderous but he was wrong. He was careless about getting the facts, careless about telling the truth, careless about his faith in God's protection and careless about his wife's honour and dignity.

Abraham had to see that he was entirely wrong to have had such suspicions. They were entirely without justification. He has to pray for the people whom he had wronged and when he prays for them, they receive healing.

3. The fact that the barren wives of Abimelech receive healing is odd, because Abraham has been praying for his own barren wife for twenty years and more. **Abraham again has to learn the sovereignty of God's ways and especially of His timing**. Evidently Abraham could pray for others' wives but prayer for his own wife was not answered! God is sovereign in giving His gifts. Every kind of gift is given *'as He wills'* (1 Corinthians 12:11). Even to Jesus it was said *'He delivered others ... let Him deliver Himself ... '*. This ought to warn us away from 'taking by faith' blessings that maybe God is not giving! Even in the greatest miracles we have to submit to the will of God. We cannot 'take' miracles or switch on God's blessings at will.

What is also noticeable is that when Abraham prayed for the wives of others, fairly soon after his own wife became pregnant. The chapter division is distracting. Immediately after Genesis 20:17–18 comes 21:1–2. When he prayed for others he received the very thing he prayed for himself.

# Chapter 28

## The Flesh and the Spirit
### (Genesis 21:1–21)

The birth of a child to Abraham and Sarah is entirely from God's grace; it is achieved by the miraculous working of God's Spirit; it is entirely a matter of God's mercy. The previous story proves it. Abraham has just disgraced himself again! He has just shown his utter weakness and his erratic wanderings from the pathway of wisdom and godliness. Yet it is at such a time God chooses to fulfil the promise.

1. **Everything connected with Isaac reminds us of the joyful grace of God**. At precisely such a time of human fallibility, Yahweh visited Sarah miraculously and sovereignly (21:1). The phrase 'Yahweh visited Sarah' speaks of a miracle. God stepped in. In the case of Ishmael, he was born according to the flesh. It required no special visitation for Ishmael to be born. But the birth of Isaac is miraculous and God's special 'visitation' is needed.

As promised and exactly on time the child is born (21:2). He is given the name 'Isaac' ('He Laughs', 21:3). It reminds us of the various times when there had been laughter about Isaac. Abraham laughed with joy when he first received God's promise about Sarah (17:17); Sarah's laughter was more in scepticism (18:12). The laughter will continue. People will chuckle with amusement at the thought of the elderly couple having such a late addition to the family! The couple will continue laughing with joy at the thought of the purpose of God going forward through the boy. And the boy himself – it is hoped – will be a happy child bringing laughter and joy to his parents. God likes laughter! Everything about Isaac expresses the joy of God's graciousness.

The boy was circumcised (21:4), in obedience to God's ruling (17:10). Circumcision marks out Abraham's community through which there will be worldwide blessing. Genesis reminds us of the great age of Abraham (21:5) and the wonderment of Sarah (21:6–7).

2. **Events connected with Ishmael remind us of self-effort and 'the flesh'.** There were perhaps two people who would have found it difficult to join in the general jubilation at the time of Isaac's birth – and they were Hagar and her teenage son, Ishmael. Ishmael had long been Abraham's much-loved favourite. Now the miraculous birth of Isaac makes it clearer than ever that Abraham's liaison with Hagar was a mistake. Abraham had at that time tried to get the promise of a child fulfilled in his own way. Now the birth of Isaac showed what God had been intending, a stunning miracle, in which God would 'visit' Sarah and produce the child. 'Through Isaac a seed shall be called into being', said God. It was now happening, and the previous attempt with Hagar was more than ever shown up for what it was.

The question now is: how will grace relate to flesh? How will the child who reminds everyone of the grace of God relate to the child who reminds everyone of a carnal incident in Abraham's life-story?

3. The answer soon becomes clear. **The flesh and the Spirit are opposed to each other**. For some time (perhaps two or three years) the child Isaac feeds at the breast. The day when he is about to be taken away from breast-feeding altogether is made into a special day (21:8). But Ishmael (who must be at least seventeen years old) is often mocking and ridiculing baby Isaac (21:9, 'playing' or 'laughing at' is not a strong enough translation; the verb here has the sense of malice and insult).

At this time Sarah requests a separation between the two children, and asks that Hagar and her son Ishmael should be sent away (21:10). Abraham is unhappy about it but agrees to her request (21:11). God promises that personally Ishmael will be blessed by God (21:12–13). The two are sent away (21:14). Hagar soon loses her way. The water runs out while they are travelling through the wilderness, and soon Hagar is convinced that her son is about to die (21:15–16). God hears her cry of distress (21:17–18) and renews His promise to Ishmael (21:17–18). She is guided to water and they survive. Ishmael grows up to be a rough but capable warrior and marries a girl from his mother's homeland (21:19–21).

The story is used by Paul to illustrate the fact that the Spirit and the flesh are always in opposition. The privileges and blessings that were bestowed on Isaac only caused jealousy and dislike on the part of Ishmael. So 'the flesh', impatient, self-seeking, unbelieving human nature, is always irritated by and opposed to the Spirit, the miracle-working, kindly, gracious working of God.

Ishmael despised Isaac. The flesh hates the Spirit. The world hates the church. Jealousy hates laughter.

The opposition has to be accepted. To follow the Spirit involves resisting the flesh. The malice of the world towards those who truly live lives of spirituality and godliness has to be accepted as a reality.

One aspect of the flesh is preoccupation with law. 'Cast out Hagar!' said Paul – meaning throw away trust in self-centred and self-confident law-keeping as a way of reaching into the heights of godliness.

If we leave aside Ishmael as a picture of 'the flesh' and consider him in and of himself, we have to say he was the object of God's mercy. When he was desperate God stepped into his life and had mercy on him. He may not have had a place in God's covenant as Isaac did. He may have **symbolised** the impatience and carnality of Abraham, but in himself, he and Hagar experienced God's mercy. For the sake of Abraham God blessed him.

We may be rough characters, with no great central place in the purpose of God, but when we cry out to God in distress – as Hagar and Ishmael did – God will hear us no matter who we are!

# Chapter 29

## God's Encouraging Hints
### (Genesis 21:22–34)

The promise concerning 'the seed' has taken a major step forward, but now there is another matter, the promise of the land. There were 'Philistines' in Israel at this time. They were not those known from later days, but were apparently an earlier group that had come from the Mediterranean area. At one stage Abraham had dug wells in an area which Abimelech the Philistine ruler regarded as his. Abraham was taking some steps towards occupying the land God had promised him. But then Abimelech's servants had seized the wells. At that time they regarded him as an alien from Haran who had no right to claim the use of any land, not even water wells! It was all very discouraging.

But suddenly there is a change. At the celebration of the weaning of Isaac, Abimelech the Philistine leader and Phicol the commander of his army were present as visitors and approached Abraham with a request (21:22a). They were so impressed with the obvious success of Abraham (21:22b) that they wanted to enter into a covenant-relationship with him. They ask Abraham to swear an oath. It seems to be a two-way covenant, because both men are involved in oath-taking (see 21:31). Abraham swears not to 'deal falsely' with them; loyalty is an essential part of covenant-relationship. They want him to 'show kindness'; kindness and favour is also part of a covenant-relationship (21:23).

Abraham joins in the oath as they wish (21:24), but he has a complaint. If the two men are to be in covenant together, he has a request. Abimelech's servants have taken a well that he dug. Abimelech is apologetic, declares his innocence, and is ready to settle the dispute (21:25–26).

So the covenant is made. Abraham gives gifts to Abimelech (21:27) but he gives seven more sheep than Abimelech expects (21:28). They are a special gift to go with the special request that Abraham's well should be recognized as his (21:29–30). The request is accepted (21:31), and the men swear a two-way oath there, or we could say they swear two oaths. So well-known was the event in later years, the place became known as 'Beer-Sheba' – the 'Well of the Oath'. Then the two visitors went home (21:32). Abraham plants a tree which will in later years give plenty of shade and by the tree builds an altar. Beersheba will be a sacred spot with a place of prayer and of sacrifice built by Abraham (21:33). He stayed in that part of the land for a long time (21:34).

1. **God gives us encouragements as we are moving in the direction of inheriting the promises**. The main point of this little story is to show us that Abraham is making some steps towards getting the promises of God fulfilled. He had been promised a seed, and Isaac has been born. He had been promised land, and now some leading men of the land of Canaan recognize that Abraham has had a certain amount of success in the land of Canaan. They talk about *'the country where you are living as an alien'*. They know that Abraham does not really belong in Canaan. He comes from Haran, and he does not have Canaanite ways. Yet they recognize that Abraham is being blessed by his God. And so they want a good relationship with him. So they accept his residence in the land and they leave him with the use of the water-wells. It is not much but it is a step towards inheriting the promises.

All of this means that we ought to take notice when small things happen to us that take a step towards inheriting what we know to be God's will for our lives. God is still alive. He still gives us intimations of His will. He still gives us encouragements along the way.

2. **The event which gave Abraham encouragement leads him into a new grasp of the character of God**. He now uses a new name for God, 'El Olam', the 'Everlasting God'. There are five compound-names for God in the book of Genesis with

the word *El* in them, *El Shaddai*, *El Elyon*, *El Olam*, *El Ro'i*, *El Bethel*. Each of these names arose in the context of some event which gave the person concerned a fresh glimpse of God. Here Abraham thinks of the distant future. Will the land that he has been promised ever belong to him? Perhaps not because he is now getting elderly. It seems that he is only getting a few small privileges such as the use of the water-wells he had dug. But that is not much. But – he thinks to himself – God is the 'Everlasting God'. When Abraham has left this world, God will still be there. The promise to him has spoken of a vast nation and of many kings coming from his 'seed'. This must mean that the promise extends out into the vast future ahead of him and ahead of his lifetime. Will Canaan ever belong to his seed? Yes! God is El Olam – the everlasting God. His plans come about slowly, but God is over and above the ages of time. He looks back and He looks ahead with perfect knowledge of what His plans are and what He is going to do.

It was some such thinking along these lines that led Abraham into a deeper knowledge of God. One little encouragement from God – a couple of neighbouring commanders turning up at a feast for his son – and Abraham is led to rejoice and know that God is the Everlasting God. Such small events in our lives can bring us such great encouragement, if we are awake to the hints of God.

# Chapter 30

## The Test of Obedience

(Genesis 22:1–2)

In Genesis chapter 22 we come to the high-point and pinnacle of the entire story of Abraham. It is at this point that the covenant which began in Genesis 15 is at last fulfilled. The promises had been first given in Genesis 12:1–3, and had been twice renewed before there was any mention of a covenant (12:7; 13:14–17). Then God started covenant-procedures at the heart of which were the same promises (15:5, 7, 13–21) but it is clear that the final oath had not been given. The covenant had yet to be 'established' (17:2). The promise was still on offer (17:4–8). The sign of circumcision was added in Genesis 17:9–14, and the promises were confirmed (17:15–16). Abraham continued to receive encouraging and increasingly detailed predictions (18:10, 14). Then at long last Isaac was born. However, even after Isaac's birth there was no oath confirming with total certainty that the covenant was going forward. Abraham was still living on the promises of God but no oath had been given. Now some time after the weaning of Isaac (22:1 lets us know that some years had gone by) there comes the greatest test of Abraham's life, and when it is finished Abraham receives the oath and the promise is finally secure. God comes to Abraham and asks Abraham to sacrifice his own son.

1. **Before we experience God's oath and 'enter into rest' we are likely to face a severe test of our obedience**. The time is a few years after the weaning (22:1a); we may guess that Isaac is at least ten years old, old enough to ask intelligent questions (see 22:7). Then God 'tests' Abraham.

God saves us by sheer grace. Abraham believed God and by

110

faith – and faith only – he was justified, totally covered with a righteousness that was not his own.

God continues to deal with us in sheer grace. He restores us (as Abraham experienced God's restorations after his mistakes). In sheer grace He takes our worst blunders (such as Abraham's going to Hagar) and overrules them for good.

Yet at the same time God asks us willingly and voluntarily to 'walk before Him' and get every area of our life right (see 17:1–2). He still deals with us in great mercy sometimes giving us our greatest blessings after our worst mistakes (as Genesis 21 follows 20:8–18).

However all along the way God is wanting us to get to a high level of obedience. If a person cleanses himself from every sin he gets to be a utensil that God will greatly use. He becomes *'sanctified, useful to the Master, fit for every good work'* (see 2 Timothy 2:21). God does much for us even without our sanctification, but God likes us to get to high levels of godliness before He gives us life's greatest blessings. Then His 'oath of mercy' might come to us. Although we have got to where we are by the continuing grace of God, and even God's rewards are a matter of grace, yet it is also true that God likes to reward us. He likes to lead us into radical, extreme, daring, obedience.

So we must not be surprised if before we experience God's oath and 'enter into rest' we discover that we are being severely tested.

2. **God's test may make no sense to us**. It seemed weird and extreme for God to ask Abraham to sacrifice Isaac. If anyone came to us today and said 'God has told me to sacrifice my son', we would say 'That wasn't God; that was the devil', and we would be right! It is true that – in the end – God was not asking for human sacrifice. God stopped the procedure before it came to its end. There is no tolerance of human sacrifice anywhere in the Bible.

But God wants to see what we are really like, how obedient we are willing to be. God seeks to discover what is in our hearts and whether we really will keep His specific command to us or not (see something similar in Exodus 16:4, and another example under the Mosaic law in Deuteronomy 8:2).

People who today think that God is asking them to do something criminal would rightly be taken as in need of psychiatric help. God's commands are appropriate to the age in which we live, and we no longer live in the days of Abraham when child-sacrifice was thought to be great devotion to God! Still, God's test might well be extremely painful and it might well make no sense to us.

3. **God's test may well seem to involve the sacrifice of everything we have lived for**. It was amazing that God should demand the sacrifice of young Isaac. For more than thirty years God had been promising 'a seed' to Abraham. It had been a stormy pathway. Sometimes Abraham was greatly daring, sometimes greatly doubting. Sometimes it was great faith, sometimes great failure. And yet Abraham had come through it all and at last Isaac had been born. But now God is asking Abraham to throw it all away! Everything for which he has lived for decades! Was the miraculous birth of Isaac to the elderly Sarah all for nothing? If Abraham loses Isaac it is not likely that Sarah will have another child! She was ninety-nine before; now she is one hundred and nine or more! How can God ask Abraham throw away what he has been waiting for all his life? Sometimes the supreme test of our faith will be a matter of putting obedience to God above something we have lived for all of our lives. Sometimes it will be to bring a phase of ministry to an end that we have been thoroughly enjoying for years and years. Sometimes it will involve doing something that might to everyone else seem foolish and ridiculous.

But before the greatest blessing of our life comes, there is likely to be a test of our obedience.

# Chapter 31

## Obeying God

(Genesis 22:3–19)

Abraham obeyed God. When God's test came he obeyed immediately, radically, totally, unquestioningly. How obedient are you willing to be to God? How obedient am I willing to be? It is a searching question.

Abraham arose early the next day, took Isaac and two assistants, got the items ready that were needed for the sacrifice and started out for the land of Moriah (22:3). On the third day he could see Mount Moriah (22:4). It was a prominent hill in the area that would one day be called Jerusalem. The *'hill of Yahweh'* (22:14) is the same place as *'the hill of Yahweh'* mentioned in Psalm 24:3 and which is used as a symbol of the people of God in Isaiah 2:2 (*'the hill of the house of Yahweh'*). 2 Chronicles 3:1 tells us that the temple would be built on this very spot. It is also in the same area as the 'Salem' of Genesis 14:18. It is the place where Melchizedek was a great high priest for his people.

The entire passage is a famous one. Jewish scholars call it the 'the Akedah' ('the Binding') recalling the point where Isaac was tied to the altar.

1. **Obedience is to be seen in a supreme sacrifice**. What does it mean to be obedient? Often it will involve putting God above something or someone that is supremely precious to us. Isaac was the most precious thing Abraham had, the one in whom all his hopes were centred. Everything for which Abraham had lived for decades of his life were tied up in his beloved son. Is he really so willing to obey God that he will not spare his own son but will deliver him up to sacrifice?

Abraham is willing to obey God, no matter what it costs

113

him. At this point Abraham leaves behind the servants (22:5). No one can help him in this part of what he has to do.

The sacrifice is to be a *'whole burnt offering'* (22:6). Abraham has the wood, and a container in which there are coals of fire, and a knife which he intends to use at the moment of sacrifice (22:6). Then there comes a painful moment. *'Where is the lamb for the burnt offering?'*, asks Isaac (22:7). It was a question that must have driven home to Abraham the pain of what it was he was doing. But God helps him and he gives an answer which is true but evasive (22:8), and the two proceed on their way.

2. **Obedience gets tested**. The whole procedure is drawn out. It has taken days to get to Moriah. Then Abraham has to climb the hill. Then he has to build the altar (22:9). Along the way Isaac has asked him a painful question. The entire procedure is prolonged. This means that Abraham is being faced with the temptation to back away from what he is doing. It is easy to 'resolve' to obey God but the test is whether one continues when the difficulties and sufferings come, and all of the implications of obedience become plain. Abraham continues hour by hour, persisting in following through in everything that will be involved in what God has asked from him. He is not just 'willing' to be obedient; he is being obedient! He does not know that there will be any release from what he is about to do. He persuades Isaac to get on the altar, and ties him there. Perhaps he explains to Isaac what has to happen. Isaac is suffering as well as Abraham. Abraham is following through in obeying God to the very end. He takes the knife in his hand (22:10) and is about to perform the act of slaughter upon his own son.

3. **Obedience gets rewarded**. At the very last moment, the angel cries from the sky. *'Abraham, Abraham!'* (22:11). It is one of the few places in Scripture where a name is called twice (see Acts 9:4 and a few others). The angel releases Abraham from the terrible slaughter he was just about to perform. *'Now I know that you fear God, since you have not withheld your son, your only son from Me'* (22:12). Soon God provides a sacrifice as a substitute for the son who was about to die (22:13). The place becomes known as 'Yahweh Yireh' – 'the LORD will see

to it', and when the story of what has happened becomes known a proverb comes into being. *'In the mount of Yahweh it will be provided'* (22:14).

Then there comes another distinct word from the angel. *'By myself I have sworn . . .'*. This is what everything in the story of Abraham has been leading to. God takes an oath and the promise is finally inherited. He has got it. God has sworn and will not change His mind. The forward movement of salvation through the seed of Abraham is now certain. The promise is being given to Abraham. From now on it will be overpowering, irresistible, unalterable, uncancellable, unchangeable.

**The sacrifice of Isaac pointed to God's surrender of His own Son**. God did what Abraham was released from doing. Romans 8:32 says *'He that spared not His own Son, but delivered Him up for us all, how shall He not also with him freely give us all things?'* It is no accident that it is using the very language of Genesis 22:16. God held nothing back. God was (so to speak) 'obedient' to the demands of the situation when He delivered him up to the power of darkness (Luke 22:53).

Just as Abraham and Isaac were alone in their sufferings, since the servants had been sent away, so God and His Son were alone in the transaction which took place on the cross. *'He took up our infirmities . . . carried our sorrows . . . We regarded him as abused . . . smitten by God, and afflicted'* (Isaiah 53:4).

# Chapter 32

## God's Oath
### (Genesis 22:1–19)

**Abraham's obedience to God was not forced obedience but voluntary obedience**. Sometimes in the Christian life there can be forced obedience. Paul says that he *'suffered the loss of all things'* (Philippians 3:8). He lost everything, but it was not that he lost it voluntarily. He **suffered** the loss of all things; it was imposed upon him. Similarly the loss of Job (in Job chapters 1 and 2) was not a matter of his surrendering his family, his wealth, his home and eventually his health. These things were **forcibly** taken from him.

It is a different matter when we do the sacrificing ourselves. Paul in Philippians 3 as well as a past tense (*'I suffered the loss...'*) could also use a present tense: *'I am counting all things to be rubbish ... in order that I may gain Christ'* (Philippians 3:8). In Philippians 2:7 we read that Jesus **humbled Himself**. It was not simply that the Father humbled Him. He humbled Himself.

In the Christian life we are sometimes willing that God should take something from us. 'Lord, if this is not your will take it from me...', we might pray. But the event in Genesis 22 was not simply a matter of Abraham's accepting what God might do to him (*'The Lord has taken away ... Blessed be the name of the Lord'*). He was willing himself to do the 'taking away'! God led him into this. In a sense he might say 'I had no choice', yet he did have a choice. This obedience of Abraham was voluntary obedience, not forced obedience. He had to walk the journey to Moriah, he had to climb the hill, he had to tie his own son upon the altar, he had to take up the knife himself. Jesus said *'If any person is willing to follow me, let him*

116

*deny himself and take up his cross...'.* Jesus wants **willing** obedience. He can force things upon us – and sometimes He does that. But when we willingly deny ourselves and when we **ourselves** take up something that is a painful sacrifice for us, we have reached a higher level of obedience. Of course I am referring to something that God Himself leads us into. We must not make foolish and dramatic sacrifices simply to prove how obedient we are. We have to be led into these things by God Himself, and we have to be sure of His will.

**Abraham's being tested by God came when he was ready**. I wonder whether Abraham could have passed this test at an earlier stage in his relationship to God. I doubt it. At least thirty-five years have gone by since Abraham left Haran. There was a twenty-four year time-gap between Genesis 12:4 and 17:1, and then another year before Isaac was born. Now Isaac is perhaps about ten years old or more. Abraham has been believing God's promises for at least 35 years.

We may say 'If God asked something like sacrificing my own son, I could not do it'. Maybe in his earlier years Abraham would have said the same thing. God did not test Abraham in this way until he knew that Abraham was ready for it. We may be able to think of things which we could not 'give up' for God, but we do not have to be theoretical about this. God's tests will come when we are ready. In the event His help will be there, and we may find that when the time comes God's grace is greater than anything we imagined. We may discover that we can pass God's tests after all.

**When Abraham reached this level of obedience he was rewarded by God's covenant-oath**. The high point of the covenant was reached. Something went forward in Abraham's relationship with God at this point. God said *'Now I know...'*, *'At this time I know...'*. The language is human language. God knows everything! But it is a way of expressing the fact that a forward step has been taken in the relationship between God and Abraham. He has reached a high point of obedience; he has passed a supreme test.

At this point God takes an oath. What does it mean for God to take an oath? The phrase *'After these things'* in

Genesis 22:1 lets us know that a very distinct event is happening in the life of Abraham. It is what James called being *'justified by works'*. *'Was not Abraham justified by works* **when he offered up Isaac?'** (James 2:21). And when was that? Thirty-five years after he had been *'justified by faith'*! This is not Abraham's becoming 'saved'; it is his reaching a high point in his relationship with God where God Himself lets Abraham know that He is pleased with him. *'At this time I know ... '*, says God (22:12). There was a specific occasion when something new happened in Abraham's life that had never happened before. It was his experience of the oath of God.

The best way to understand the oath of God is to ask the questions 'Can God change His mind? Can He withdraw a promise? Can He withdraw a threat?' The answer is that God is often represented as 'changing His mind'. Maybe it is only a way of talking, but if so it is a 'way of talking' that we are allowed to use. In Genesis 22:16 Abraham definitively receives the promise. At this point the climax of the covenant-relationship is reached. The promise is received in a way that cannot be lost. Before this point Abraham could have forfeited the promise (as Saul forfeited kingship). After God's oath the promise cannot be lost (just as the promise to David could not be abolished after 2 Samuel 7). Abraham 'entered into rest'. The promise had been 'obtained' (Hebrews 6:12). From this point on it was certain that Jesus would be the seed of Abraham.

# Chapter 33

## Entering Into Rest
### (Genesis 22:1–19)

Let us pursue further this matter of the 'oath of God'.

1. **The case of the Israelites in the wilderness was that of an oath of wrath**. God promised to give Israel the promised land, but they refused to believe, and rebelled again and again. Finally God took an oath. In Numbers 14 they grumble in disbelief once more, refusing to believe that God can give them the promised land. Moses intercedes for them (Numbers 14:13–19). God had sworn on oath that He would give the land to Israel (Numbers 14:16). God replies. He **will** forgive them (Numbers 14:20), but He will take an oath that **that** generation will not enter Canaan. For **that** generation the promise has been withdrawn. God has 'changed His mind' about that generation. He takes an oath (Numbers 14:21–23), swearing that that generation will never enter Canaan.

After the oath has been taken no change can take place. The Israelites **now** resolve to go into Canaan (Numbers 14:40) but it is too late. It could have been done yesterday but it cannot be done today.

The oath is the point where the matter is settled; after the oath no change can take place.

2. **The case of Saul was that of an oath of wrath**. God can withdraw a promise. God chose Saul to be the king of Israel. His line *'would have lasted for ever'* (1 Samuel 13:14) but there came a point where Saul sinned so severely that God 'changed His mind' and rejected Saul from being king (1 Samuel 15:26). It is **after** this event that it is said that *'He is not a man that He should change His mind'* (1 Samuel 15:29).

119

The oath is the point where the matter is settled; after the oath no change can take place.

3. **The case of Nineveh was that of a situation where no oath has been taken**. Jonah told the city of Nineveh that in forty days' time God would destroy the city (Jonah 3:4). Yet the king of Nineveh said *'Who knows? God may turn around and change His mind and withdraw His burning anger...'* (Jonah 3:9). He was right! 'God changed his mind concerning the calamity which He had declared He would bring...' (Jonah 3:10).

When no oath has been taken a change can take place. Promises can be lost; threats can be averted.

4. **The case of the high-priest after the order of Melchizedek is one where an oath of mercy has been given**. The letter to the Hebrews points out that the priests in the order of Levi *'became priests without an oath'* (Hebrews 7:21). God could abolish the levitical priesthood because He had not taken any oath that it would continue for ever. But in the case of the *'priest after the likeness of Melchizedek'* there was an oath. *'The Lord has sworn and will not change His mind'* (Hebrews 7:21; Psalm 110:4). The reason why God abolished the levitical order of priests but does not abolish the priestly work of Jesus is that He has taken an oath. God **cannot** withdraw the priesthood of Jesus since He has taken an oath.

Again, we note, the oath is the point where the matter is settled; after the oath no change can take place.

The Christian is in covenant with God. There is a relationship in which God is our Father and we are His children. 'Covenant' is a promise which has an oath added to it. As soon as we come to salvation we are God's children but we will not experience the oath of God straightaway. God's covenant is His **offer** of an 'oath of generosity' (there are different kinds). We are not under the Mosaic law which was a different kind of covenant altogether.

The climax of the covenant is when God takes an oath and the Christian 'enters into rest'. At such a time he has secured God's promises to him. He is powerfully fulfilling his life's calling. His work for God cannot be overthrown. It is certain that the promise is coming. It is supremely restful. God pours out abundance of blessing.

For the Christian the covenant goes forward on the basis of sacrifice. He lives daily on the blood of Jesus which gives him eternal redemption (*'having obtained eternal redemption'*, Hebrews 9:12), daily cleansing (*'How much more **will** the blood ... cleanse your conscience?'*, Hebrews 9:14) and makes it possible to obtain our reward, the oath of God (*'Those who have been called **may** receive the promise...'*, Hebrews 9:15). The tenses in Hebrews 9:12, 14 and 15 are significant. Redemption **has been** obtained; cleansing **is being** daily obtainable; inheritance **may be** reached.

A covenant of generosity is unconditional after it has been given. The oath is given after faith and patience, maybe many years after our first salvation. When God swears in His mercy, His promises of achieving the *'good works ordained that we should walk in them'* has been obtained and cannot be lost.

Covenant is designed to encourage and to motivate. God offers the blessing of His oath to us, and invites us to pursue it. All Christians are *'children of Abraham'*. We follow in the footsteps of our father. We too are in covenant with God. God is wanting to say to us also *'Now I know that you fear me'* and pour out abundant blessings upon us in which we *'enter into rest'* and inherit God's promises.

**The experience of the oath of God involves a direct witness from God,** or (as the New Testament might say) a direct witness of the Holy Spirit. God did not say to **Himself**, 'Now I know that Abraham fears me...' (contrast Genesis 22:12). He said **to Abraham** *'Now I know that you fear me..."* (Genesis 22:12). God lets us know His will. He gives us gifts of His Spirit. He gives us a calling and a ministry. By faith and patience, like Abraham, we pursue His will. The greatest day of our life comes when we inherit what He is promising to do in us and through us. When He says *'I swear I will bless...'*, we enter into rest.

# Chapter 34

## Rest or Retirement?
### (Genesis 22:1–24)

In Genesis 22 it is not the **reality** of Abraham's faith that is being tested. Long before Abraham's being called to sacrifice his son he had shown that his faith was real. *'Against hope but in hope Abraham believed in order that he would become a father of many nations...'* (Romans 4:18). Everything had seemed against Abraham. Yet he was confident that the child would come and that he would indeed be the father of many nations. Abraham's faith was real enough. What is being tested is how far he will go, how far his faith will take him in obedience to God.

This test came just after a great blessing, *'After these things'* (22:1). Abraham had just received his encouragement concerning his inheriting the land when this great test came. It should not surprise us if the greatest testings come after the greatest blessing.

This test led him to reckon that God was able even to raise Isaac from the dead (see Hebrews 11:19). God had said that Abraham's line would go forward through Isaac, yet here was God asking Abraham to sacrifice his son. One can see the things that Abraham would be asking himself: 'How can my line of descendants go forward if God is asking me to sacrifice my son? How can God keep His word if He is asking me to sacrifice Isaac?' He came to the conclusion there was only one way in which it could be done. It must mean that God would raise Isaac from the dead. This is the point of Hebrews 11:19. It was through the way Abraham faced this trial that his faith was enlarged. Because he was willing to obey God it had the effect of enlarging his faith and leading him to believe even in the resurrection. This is why in Genesis 22:5 Abraham says *'We will return'*. He expected Isaac to come back. He was believing that after he sacrificed his son God would have to raise Isaac from the dead. He was believing in resurrection.

Abraham's faith was enlarged in another way. The New Testament says that Abraham saw Jesus' day (John 8:56). He caught a glimpse of the coming of Jesus. When and how did this happen? Surely it was here more than anywhere. Abraham takes his son and he is willing not to withhold him but to deliver him over to sacrifice. He is about to make the sacrifice when suddenly God provides the sacrifice instead! A lamb dies in the place of one who was condemned. The sacrifice that God provided was the substitute for the one who was about to die. In this event Abraham surely glimpses dimly what God would do. He had been through the experience of not sparing his own son. God had provided a sacrifice, but one day God would provide His own Son to be the lamb of sacrifice. Abraham saw the basic ingredients of the death and resurrection of the Son of God when he experienced the near-death of Isaac, and got Isaac back from the dead.

When you are tested by God and you pass the test you will discover more of God. You will see more of God's ways. You will see into the heart of God and will discover His sympathy and find out how much He is willing to stand by you. Above all you will see Jesus as the One who dies for you.

Finally God enlarges the promise more than ever. He again puts the promise of great numerical increase to Abraham. His seed will be vast, like *'the stars of heaven'*, like *'the sand ... on the seashore'*. The promise is finally sure and settled not just because of Abraham's faith but because of Abraham's obedience. His salvation was by faith only. But it was by faith and patience that he got to this high level of obedience, and because he obeyed God's voice he inherited God's promises.

So Abraham has *'entered into rest'* but there are even further steps of faith that have to be taken. 'Entering into rest' is not a synonym for finishing one's life work. There is more for Abraham yet! Abraham is now elderly. Was it now time to 'retire' from the life of faith? He had accomplished the supreme calling of his life. At this very point, Abraham is tempted to withdraw from his call to Canaan. Abraham is not beyond temptation and at this point he gets a hint that he might like to return home to Haran. For many years he had not been in contact with his relatives but now someone reported to Abraham that his family in Haran in far-away Mesopotamia were doing well (22:20–24). He had nephews and nieces in Haran that he had never seen. It was a piece of information he would soon make use of – the Rebekah of 22:23 became his son's wife – but it must have come to him as a temptation. He had no land in Canaan. He was elderly. The promise of a seed had been achieved. He knew from now on the progress of 'the seed' could not be stopped.

These insignificant verses have always meant a lot to me personally. I was born in Britain but have spent most of my life in Africa. Years ago I received an invitation to become pastor of a church in Britain. It was a large and influential church and for various reasons I found it a very tempting offer. One verse of Scripture held me from turning aside from what God had called me to do. I happened to be working through Genesis and I had reached Genesis 22:20–24. It did not seem a very inspiring passage but I read Hebrews 11:15 *'If indeed they had been thinking of that country from which they went out, they would have had opportunity to return'*! I knew it was the voice of God for me, and I said 'No' to the congregation in Britain. I have stayed in Africa ever since.

It was a time in Abraham's life when he was thinking of that country from which he went out, and he had opportunity to return! He kept in touch with his distant relatives but he did not go back to Canaan. His future was with Canaan, not with Mesopotamia.

# Chapter 35

## Glory That Lasts For Ever
### (Genesis 23:1–20)

Abraham still has one more great lesson to learn. He has entered into rest and the success of his life's work is assured. Now he has to face the challenge of inheritance beyond the grave. The ultimate blessing for the believer is after this life, in 'the world to come'. It is not just a matter of preoccupation with this world. It is true that God gives us many blessings and takes care of us in this world. But they are just extras and side-effects added on top of what God is doing for us. The Christian also has his eyes fixed on what is to be his or hers beyond the grave.

God had given Abraham promises about a land. He was to go to 'the land' that God would show him. *'All this land will I give to you'*, God said again and again. But at this point Abraham is elderly. His life will obviously soon be over and he has not received any land.

It was forcefully brought home to him when Sarah died. She died near Hebron (23:1–2) which was one of the places where Abraham had stayed. He and Sarah had some kind of temporary home there. Abraham had not received any territory. The promise that had been coming again and again has not been fulfilled in this respect. In the New Testament Paul speaks of the promise that Abraham should inherit **the world** (Romans 4:13). God was not just speaking about the limited territory of Canaan when He gave these promises to Abraham. Later, the nation of Israel did indeed get that territory. But Canaan was only a tiny part of what God was intending to give. In Hebrews 11:8 it says Abraham sojourned in the land of promise as in a foreign land. He was looking forward *'to a city which has foundations whose builder and maker is God'* (11:10). The land Abraham was looking for was not purely and entirely in this world. Canaan was only the first instalment, and Abraham himself would not get any of it. The real territory was the whole world. The seed of Abraham will inherit the earth. There will be a new heavens and new earth in which righteousness dwells. The ultimate hope of the Christian is a glorified earth, when Christians will have new bodies and live in a glorified earth. The ultimate hope is heaven on earth.

When Sarah dies none of the land belongs to Abraham and he does not even have land enough to bury his wife in. He has to go to some Hittites to ask for a place to bury her. Yet the promise has been all about land and physical territory.

Often Christians act as if being a Christian is just a kind of insurance policy to save us from hell and make sure that we have a good life here on planet earth. But this is not the right way of looking at salvation at all. We must not act as if God's blessings for us are entirely in this world. Peter said *'Do not be surprised at the fiery ordeal ... as though something strange were happening'* (1 Peter 4:12). Jesus said *'In the world you shall have tribulation'* (John 16:33). We are not to expect an easy life. Our sights are to be set on glory beyond the grave. We are looking for a new heavens and new earth. We are looking for the world to come, a city which has foundations. Abraham wanted Canaan but the Canaan which God had in mind was a spiritual matter and the last phase of it was to be obtained in the world beyond this his lifetime.

Abraham knew that God's purpose would continue even after he had died. He wants to bury Sarah in Canaan. He goes to the Hittites and asks to buy some property (23:3–4). The Hittites offer to give Abraham the land he needs (23:5–6) but Abraham is not happy with that. He wants to buy it in a legal way. He buys it at 'the gate' which was the place where business was done (23:7–16). He wants this plot of land to be legally owned by his family. He knows that the future of the purpose of God is tied up with what God will do in Canaan. So he wants Sarah buried there and he wants that patch of ground to belong to his family. Everyone will know in ages to come that Abraham believed that his descendants would own that land. So the land becomes Abraham's (23:17–20), an indication that Abraham had faith in what God would do beyond his lifetime.

Are you living for this world? For pleasure? Money? Property? The thing to live for is God's purpose in history through the seed of Abraham, Jesus. Then you become an heir of the new heavens and the new earth in which righteousness dwells. Life rushes by at such a fast rate. We are to live for the world which is to come. Abraham had no fear of death.

The purposes of God will go on beyond our personal death. But we shall not lose the land. We shall have a new earth and we shall radiate in glory in God's new world.

In Abraham's life story we have a preview of the Christian life. It begins with justifying faith. Our call to salvation is at the same time a call to ministry and inheritance. We get caught up into God's plan and we become co-workers with Christ. The whole story of our life will be the story of the conflicts and triumphs of faith. Faith is the master-characteristic of the Christian life. It leads into every other blessing. By faith and patience we inherit God's promises for our lives. We achieve something within His kingdom. As we live the life of faith we are all along the way in covenant relationship with Him. God has sworn that Abraham's seed will come into being. He has sworn that His Priest after the order of Melchizedek will continue to intercede. We have Jesus as the anchor of our souls. We are tied to Him and He is in glory.

We live depending on the oath to Abraham. The seed of Abraham cannot fail. But we are wanting our own oath. We are children of Abraham and we want God to swear to us as He swore to Abraham. If we persist it will happen. He will say 'Now I know you fear me'. Most of our life after that point will be reaping more than sowing. Yet final glory never comes in this life. Our Canaan, our promised land, is partly here and now. We get a good portion of it even now and our life flows with 'milk and honey'. Yet the best is yet to come. We are laying up treasure in heaven. Any part of 'Canaan' here is only a first instalment. We already have a bit of heaven below and soon will get heaven above. Soon we shall pass on to the next phase of our inheritance and our Isaac will get married and continue the life of faith without us. We shall be happy to have it that way, for we shall be appreciating the city which has foundations, whose maker and builder is God. We shall be enjoying the glory that lasts for ever.